Soul To The World

A Lightworker's Transformational Journey

Jennifer Terese Haag

For permission, please email Jennifer Haag at soultotheworld@gmail.com

ISBN: 979-8-9899345-0-8 (paper)

ISBN: 979-8-9899345-1-5 (digital)

ISBN: 979-8-9899345-2-2 (Hardback)

Cover Photo by Oleksandr P

Cover Design by Aubrey Labitigan: facebook.com/designjai

Author Picture by Stella Lopez-Mochel

First Edition, February 2024

Printed in the United States of America

DEDICATION

I dedicate this book to my children,
David, Conor and Rose.
For you are the future
and will carry my Soul forever...

~TESTIMONIALS~

"*Soul To The World* is riveting – full of delightful imagery, practical insight and spiritual wisdom. A must-read to assist with your awakening process!" -Sarah K Grace, Author of *Journey Into Grace, Tales of a Psychic Paramedic*

"*Soul To The World* is an engaging read – part biography, part masterclass in how to find your Light. As you delve into Jennifer's journey, you'll navigate a life brimming with joy and hope shining brightly through trauma and challenges. This book is guaranteed to help all spiritual seekers learn and benefit from her journey." ~Charles Gibson, Intuitive Business Coach and Entrepreneur

TABLE OF CONTENTS

~INTRODUCTION~

In this book, I use my own life journey, generational and personal healing, and soul lessons, to illustrate how the reader can recognize and achieve their own spiritual transformation from buried generational, childhood, and life trauma, to living present in each moment healed, consciously aware and with acceptance, peace, joy, and purpose. *Soul to the World* eloquently explains through the my own experiences why we cannot move forward on our spiritual journey to Oneness (which is the goal of every single Soul), without identifying, forgiving, healing, and permanently letting go of our hidden wounds and trauma. Woven within this profound personal journey is practical information the reader can use to help themselves ascend to their next soul level, which is an evolutionary step for humanity and leads us to ultimately experience heaven on Earth.

We design our lives before we are born. We choose the family we are born into, the major events in our lives, our career or life path, and we fill it with important guideposts (people we meet, experiences to live through, lessons to be learned) to remind us along the way, of who we truly are, and what our life purpose is. *Every single person is undergoing a spiritual transformation, whether consciously or not.* When we are fortunate to recognize someone in the same stage of soul development, we feel an immediate rapport, resonance and spiritual connection.

I was given gifts of clairsentience, clairaudience and at times, precognition when my soul needed a nudge. I spent my youth and young adulthood looking to others for confirmation of my own intuition. When I finally recognized my soul's path, I alternated between incredible awareness and joy, and fear-based denial. How could I trust what my Soul and Higher Self were telling me? It went against everything I was raised to believe. My husband wasn't thrilled with my spiritual awakening, and my children were not getting the traditional life for which I had prepared. I was filled with incredible fear and yet my soul longed for recognition and acceptance of my life purpose.

The spiritual messages I received from my Higher Self for almost thirty years were consistent and patient (written in italics throughout this book). I was here on Earth, at this time, to be Messenger to the world, of what is to come, and hold space for those who are awakening to their True Self now and in the future.

Ten years after undergoing, accepting and healing from a dramatic Spiritually Transformative Experience

(STE), I was given a life mission by the Archangel Metatron which includes this book you now read, and recognition I am a Soul Healer. I have always lived a life of service and knew I could not deny what was asked of me. I have been helping to heal souls from Fear and its negative effects my whole life.

For those on the spiritual path, we know that an increasing number of people are gradually awakening to their true selves, are discovering their life path, are living with purpose and passion, and are changing the future of our planet one incredible recognition and discovery at a time.

We are all here on Earth for a purpose. We are all part of the Plan. There can be no judgement of each other, we have lived each other's lives. Reincarnation is how the soul continues its lessons and eventual unification with Source. Fighting against and killing another, is like fighting against and killing ourselves. To transform our future into one of peace, we must have compassion, acceptance and unconditional love for each other as we each find our own way to recognition of our True Self, our Life Purpose, and realization that we are exactly where we are supposed to be at this time and place.

To reach Oneness, we must resolve all Karma, we must heal all hurts, we must forgive all who trespass against us. We must heal not just ourselves, but our ancestors. In so doing, we release ourselves of Burden and are free to become one with All, to be at peace, to be in our natural state of pure love and joy. This is Heaven on Earth and is our human destiny. I have shared my path within these pages, so you might find your own way to healing and ultimate Oneness with Source. I am here, to help make manifest this destiny, as a sixth density Being of Light. I am here for all of us, including my human self.

There is an All Knowing, Compassionate, and Creative Presence which abides within all living things. It is for you to discover, as you follow your own Way. Within these pages, I reference the All by the names 'God' or 'Source.' If you choose not to believe in the Creative Consciousness, understand that Presence resides within you, always. It is for you to discover, in time.

PART I
SOUL AWAKENING

You are going to lead many towards the light within themselves. You were chosen specifically for this life because of who you really are and have been before.

~My Higher Self, March 2007

Soul to the World

1 PROPHETIC MESSAGE

If my parents had known and shared with me, I am a gifted Empath[1], would my childhood have been easier to bear? I grew up in a boisterous loving home with music, fair discipline, love of God, of family, and a hidden generational darkness which affected us all subconsciously. A quiet observer, I noticed and reacted to nonverbal behavior and emotional energy of others, and buried truths held within each soul. I could sense and feel all of it, causing me to alternate between compassion and joy, or to hide in a ball of invisibility. I was not aware of these abilities until my mid-twenties. It is in our self-discovery and mistakes, that our soul can learn and grow.

Most of the time, my feelings and intuitive understanding didn't make sense to what was happening

---

1   An Empath (also called clairsentient) is highly attuned to the feelings and emotions of those around them. Empaths feel what another person is feeling at a deep emotional level. They are very intuitive and caring. Empaths are sensitive to the environment and are aware of sights, sounds and smells, others may not experience. Their heightened extrasensory perception can be misconstrued as mental illness.

in my environment. When I was young, I would ask for confirmation of my feelings from parents, teachers or siblings but was often told I was wrong, or that I made someone feel bad for voicing my intuition. I feel no one understood me in grade school, so was treated as different and 'separate from.' I believe they sensed my 'otherness' and that made them uncomfortable. This created a need to bully me or distance themselves physically from my presence. The daily humiliation and bullying were baffling and painful from the age of eight to fourteen. The worst part is I could sense their own confusion at their behavior towards me. My response was to become silent and move somewhere unnoticeable. By the age of ten, I was very adept at hiding my feelings, and staying in the background, out of sight and notice. After teachers shared, I often had my head in the clouds during class, my mom had me evaluated. It was determined I was very smart, thought way ahead, and had a tough time staying focused in the present moment. (These days you are medicated for that.)

As a young girl, I became obsessed with thoughts of death; of my parents, of myself, of my family...and what happens when we die. The lessons I'd learned in my Catholic school did not address this topic. Often my mom would reassure me and send me back to bed with water and a song that would soothe me back to sleep. I experienced night terrors and nightmares. I would wake screaming from what I thought were vivid hallucinations in my room.... animals who were dying, or shadowed beings hovering on my ceiling or corner of my room (I later discovered I was seeing them). I walked and talked in my sleep often. My sister would frequently tell me stories of things I had said at night or having to gently guide me back to my bed. Sometimes I would dread sleep and keep myself awake with reading until I slept from exhaustion.

Even though I was young, I'd always had an inherent sense I was here on Earth for an important purpose. I couldn't have said what it was, but an inner pull and knowing led me. I knew I had to trust it. I took courage from this awareness when life was difficult. Most of my extrasensory abilities remained latent through my childhood and high school years. This was a time of emotional trial and preparation. Unbeknownst to me, I was building the foundation of my future. I had always been a 'home hearth cricket' as my mom would say. She thought I would attend a local college, become a teacher, and settle somewhere close to home. A large part of me wanted that, but a deeper sense told me to move North. I spent the first few years after high school completing undergraduate work at a local community college. I had no thought of my future then, only that I would go away to college and hope the right career path would show up for me. I wanted to experience real weather, changing seasons and a slower pace of life, so chose Northern California. Approximately one and a half years before I transferred, I had my first vivid supernatural experience. It was something completely outside of anything I understood about myself, my religious upbringing, or my spiritual nature. In 1989[2], while folding clothes in my room one afternoon, tremendous spiritual knowledge flooded my mind. I was given a prophetic message, for myself and humanity.

> In the later middle of my life ...there would be tremendous upheaval in the world. Something would happen that would affect every single person on the planet. This "Event" (as I came to call it in my mind) would transform everything we have ever known about ourselves and our world. It was not nuclear annihilation... it would not be a physical death, but it would affect people tremendously. So many people would go into fear. People could possibly die or have a tough time because of this fear and the resistance and actions they took because of fear.

> The event was a gift to the world. A Catalyst. A new way of living and being that would transform everything we knew about being human up to that point. It was something to be anticipated with joy and excitement. We needed to have faith that all was for a purpose and... I was here to help people get through it. That I had an important mission. What was coming afterward would be so incredible. Something none of us could envision but what we all wanted.

---

2   1989 is considered a pivotal point on the world stage: Ayatollah Khomeini died, the Berlin Wall was destroyed, and the Cold War ended, healing a divided Europe. It was also the year Kryon, a group of angelic beings, contacted and began working with Lee Carroll (an author and businessman) to help support humanity's spiritual awakening.

I can't explain how tremendous it felt. The intense "knowing" that I experienced. This knowing or understanding was and is as real as any experience I'd had. I wanted to tell everyone I knew! The internet did not exist. We didn't have cell phones, YouTube, Facebook, or Wikipedia. I had no way of checking this information with anyone else. I told my mom about it. She had always been interested in what I had to say and seemed open about different experiences.

Her Irish eyebrows rose while I told her. She was quiet for a moment, and then thoughtfully replied, "so much in the world is a mystery, Jenny. You should pray about it. The answer will come to you eventually."

She also suggested I start listening to an evening radio program she liked to listen to called Coast to Coast[3] with Art Bell. One night, Art asked his audience to call in with any experience that defied explanation or was mysterious in any way. I was able to get on the show and told Art what I had experienced. After listening to me, he exclaimed how incredible it was! He told his listeners and me that he had received hundreds of similar stories! He had heard of a major event coming in our future that would change everything we had ever known. Some people had more details, like I did. After I hung up, I sat in awe. Someone else had this experience! It wasn't all in my head? He knew what I was

---

3   Coast to Coast is an AM late night radio talk show that deals with a variety of topics on the paranormal and supernatural. It was hosted by Art Bell from 1988-2002 and is now hosted by George Noory.

talking about. I was floored. Receiving outside confirmation of an intuitive message was huge for me. Eventually everyday life took over once more and I moved on, but if I ever checked within me, that event was still there...holding a static position. The older I got, the closer the "Event" felt. I let go of worry over what it might be and focused on my present. After all, my middle age seemed far away.

While in college, I discovered spiritual tools of communication such as the pendulum, muscle testing, and automatic writing. I resonated with automatic writing[4] and began using that to communicate with my inner self and spirit guides. Usually, I'd ask questions about my relationships. My Catholic upbringing condemned the use of fortune telling, so I did not ask questions about my future. Messages of the future still came. Most of the messages centered around a book I would write, and an important mission I had in the world. I had no idea what this was, so focused on school, work, and my off and on long term relationship.

DON'T I KNOW YOU?

Around the same time as the prophetic message, I began having unsettling and unexplainable experiences when I was out with friends or family, or on my own. My first conscious awareness happened around the age of 18 or 19 years old. My best girlfriend and I went to a St. Patrick's

---

4   Automatic Writing uses the non-dominate hand (initially) to ask questions of the inner unknowable Self. Works best after meditation.

Day party. We didn't know anyone but enjoyed the music and meeting new people. As we sat at a table listening to a great Irish band, a guy yelled over to me from another table. "Hey...you...come here!" I glanced over and saw he was handsome but obviously deep in his cups. My friend and I shrugged and walked over. I noticed they were all staring at me and laughing. Laughing incredulously, the guy said," You look exactly like my buddy's fiancé! He's over there.... go and pretend you are her." *Are you kidding?* Smiling sheepishly, I said no thanks and walked back to my chair.

He came over, apologized for his rudeness, and said "listen...you really look familiar. It's uncanny.... I feel like I know you...." I laughed and assured him that no, we had never met.

We left eventually because they kept calling over to us. If that had been the only time that happened, I would shrug it off as silly. Over the years, a stranger would approach me a few times a year, insisting we knew each other. It was more than casual mistaken identity. They would approach me with hesitant anticipation, ask where we had met, and when I said we had never met, would insist I was wrong... they absolutely knew me, but just couldn't remember where. I could feel how bemused they felt. After this happened about 5 or 6 times, I realized something odd was happening. It didn't happen often enough to be overly concerned, although eventually I realized it would continue. When I was in my early forty's, I attended a spiritual conference in San Mateo, California. The first day as I waited to purchase a ticket, someone in front of me turned around suddenly and questioned why they knew me. I laughed and stated I just had a familiar face. As usual, they looked me full in the face and said no, they knew me! But from where? Always, I had to reassure them, or make up a story of where we must have met...for them to feel comfortable to walk away with backward looks. During the three days of conference, the unusual occurrence happened four times with four different people! Determined to find the underlying cause of it, I went to a spiritual healer's booth and told her about my experiences of the past twenty plus years.

She studied me carefully, looked deeply into my eyes, gave a big sigh and replied, "You are a healer. You travel in your sleep to help those who seek help, whether emotional, spiritual, or psychological, and you help heal them. They recognize you at a soul level and they are grateful." She squeezed my arm gently with a knowing smile and walked away.

I supposed she meant I astral[5] traveled. I had no conscious memory of this, although I wished I did. It would take some time before I realized I wasn't meant to remember. We are allowed to consciously remember spiritual experiences if that awareness will help us in our

---

5   Astral projection or travel involves an intentional Out of Body Experience (OBE) where one's consciousness becomes a 'body of light' that functions separately from the physical body, attached by an 'umbilical cord' of light. With control and training, one can travel the 'astral plane'.

life purpose. There are many who have experienced astral projection, being out of body, and remembered Near Death Experiences, because they had made a soul contract before birth, to do so. I was later told by my Higher Self, that my missions were many, and remembering would impact me in ways that would hamper soul growth. I accepted this and moved on. That was the last time a stranger approached me. I believe I have continued this work. My guides led these people to me, so I might know my true self. As soon as I became consciously aware, the experiences stopped. As of this writing, it has been over 13 years. I have since discovered I am and have been working as a Soul Healer[6].

---

6   Soul Healing involves the Emotional Body, as described to me by my Higher Self. I support an individual soul by helping them to let go of and heal from negative emotions like fear and past emotional and spiritual trauma.

Soul to the World

2   SIGNS

In the fall of 1991, I began my bachelor's degree in Anthropology at CSU Sacramento, with an ardent desire to understand how and why we are each so different and yet so like one another. Where do we come from? Why do we wage war and kill others for ownership of land and property that is ours for such a short lifetime? Why is there such a racial and religious divide? Why do these ancient hatreds persist? I was not consciously aware of my true interest... how did humanity become so closed off to our true selves and understanding that we are all One, here for the purpose of learning and loving ourselves and one another?

Towards the end of my studies, I experienced tremendous emotional and spiritual pain from drama happening within my family and a painful experience with my ex-boyfriend. Late in the evening one chilly winter night, compelled by heartache, I climbed to the top of my college footfall bleachers. I stared East towards the High Sierras, into a velvet black sky marred by bright lights from around the university and city. Something unnamed within me cried out to God.

"Why am I here? Why is life so hard? Are you there? Am I alone? Please send me a sign...let me know I'm not alone...that I'm being guided and can trust it!"

Abruptly, a blinding white light filled the whole horizon and flashed across the sky. I was dumbfounded! Did that just happen? What was that? Of course, my analytical mind was trying to fit it into a tidy box. The next day I searched for evidence people had seen a UFO, or there was a transformer explosion, or something. No one had seen it. It was a message to me. Over the years, when I doubted my path or focus, I thought about that Light. It was unwavering, larger than life and could not be misunderstood. Source heard me. God gave me an amazing miraculous sign! I have never been alone, not even during my darkest most solitary moments.

God's messages are for all of us and are always there if you know where to look. I am visual and in desperation, demanded a visible sign from Source which was given immediately. The answer is not usually obvious or immediate. Most of the time, God's answers are subtle. Metaphorically, we ask for a blue present with a pink bow and are given a pink present with a blue bow. I think, sometimes, we need reminding on our journey. Perhaps my sign was so obvious and immediate because it was a guidepost. Perhaps I had asked ahead of time for an "Instant Message" from

God, knowing I would need reminders along my journey. In my mid to later twenties, I began receiving messages of the future during my automatic writing and meditation. It was very subtle at first, and often misunderstood by me. When insistent messages came through that I would write an important book, I often ignored it. My guides and Higher Self were very patient. As I grew spiritually, they revealed more over time.

After I graduated in 1994, I felt restless about my future. The only path with Anthropology for me was teaching which required a master's degree. I wasn't sure that was what I wanted, so took a few administrative assistant temporary jobs while I decided my next move. It is said, while doing repetitive tasks, we can go into a meditative trance and have many psychic experiences.

One day at work, I was typing or filing paperwork when unexpectedly, a spiritual download flowed through me. Infinite universal knowledge, self-awareness, understanding, jubilance, bliss, and an incredible knowing coursed through my whole body and mind. I felt compelled to write it down as fast as it came in. Before this happened, inwardly I was asking questions like, 'Are we manifesting outside of ourselves, the abilities and knowledge we already hold within? Isn't it true that whatever we are seeking, we already have within us? How do we tap into this knowledge? It's meant for every single person, not just the religious...'

'It is our given right and freedom as human beings, made in the image of God, to be able to use the knowledge and power held within each of us. There are many through the ages and today who are known as seers, priests, priestesses, storytellers, shamans, holy men and women, wise people, mystics, prophets, saints, visionaries, and more who have all tapped into some of the greatness that is held in all of us. These people are regarded with suspicion, envy, awe, and wonder. They are given names and stations in their lives which give them power. They are made to appear godlike, where they have merely tapped into what is for all of us, our human potential.

Each of us holds this power within us. We are so ingrained to believe we are only what our cultural and social world has made of us. To a degree, this is true, but not regarding our innate abilities and knowledge. From birth, we are made to forget what it is to Know and Understand and Apply. We are made to be civilized so that we might be able to someday understand all there is to know. A little backwards. For the rest of our lives, we are searching for our lost selves; our passion, trueness of being, our understanding and our "holiness."

Perhaps our spiritual guides are trying to guide us to this knowledge and its attainment. We are getting close to our spiritual selves, step by step. It would explain the great amount of literature, philosophy and spiritual ideology *which is occurring all over the world. Our awareness of our guides. What we need to do is learn how to unlock the doors, to unearth 80-90% of the brain we're not using. So many people are looking outside of themselves for the answer. Only a few know in their heart/mind/soul that the path to enlightenment and attainment of our goals is through understanding the Essence of Who we Are, How we work and What we need. All self-improvement books and tips are manifestations of our growing need for understanding. People like Deepak Chopra, Dr. Moody, Marianne Williamson, Dr. Wayne Dyer, Teilhard De Chardin, etc., have all tapped into various parts of the whole. They are trying to send out the same message. They specialize but are all parts of the Whole.*

The universe is merely an extension of our minds. The universe is a manifestation of our inner selves and the world we create for ourselves.

Occasionally, we learn something new. An answer is discovered. Here on earth, someone may come to an illuminated understanding of what/who we are as humans. The physical and spiritual world are parallel dimensions and linked to each other. We reflect on one another.

Could this idea, this wonderful miraculous thought hold the answer and reason for everything we do? Perhaps our problems/illnesses/diseases/ evilness are a reflection on our despair and hopelessness on ever attaining our enlightenment. Perhaps there is an evil 'force' that is trying to keep us away from ourselves. That force is a manifestation of our fear in its many forms.

If we look at the evolution of spirit and mind compared to our earth's development, we will find correlations. We've had the answer all along. Everyone has. Whether it is seen as light/dark, physical/non-physical, Ying/Yang, etc. It's been in front of our noses all this time! Knowing this does not mean we stop trying to learn and understand our world and place in it, but it means bringing an understanding and realization of where each of us are coming from with acceptance.'

Our soul chooses our moment of Awakening before birth. We have no control over when it happens, although we have free will to accept or ignore it, at least for a time. Eventually, our soul's path will reinsert itself in our consciousness. My prophetic vision was the first spark, this was the second.

Awakening[7] is a term that has been used over and over in society, without knowledge or an intuitive understanding of what it really means. When we awaken, we remember who we really are as eternal spiritual beings

---

7   For a thorough listing of spiritual awakening symptoms, you can research online. We are each undergoing a personal experience, but there are commonalities. They can occur in any order. Please see Resources at the end of this book for more information.

housed temporarily in physical bodies. For those who have awakened, we are now in a state of Remembering our True Selves and are consciously participating in the unfoldment of our life purpose. In the initial stages of our awakening, we become aware of the illusion of separateness we are taught from birth. There is no true separation. Our ego is broken down and subjected to intense scrutiny, where we then compassionately let go of lifelong expectations and trust the unfolding of our life, as it is meant to be. When we awaken, our whole mind, body, and soul is affected. We become aware of lies being sold as truth in society. We give a hard look at relationships in our life, our careers, and our goals, and often find them lacking authenticity. We slowly begin changing to align to our inner truth which holds steady. Our partner, spouse, family, friends, and co-workers are often upset when we start to change. Many relationships and careers do not survive. For many, our first compulsion when we sense a disturbance in the 'force,' is to run and hide. Such was the case for me.

Soul to the World

3   DENIAL AND ILLNESS

In 1997, I went back to school for a Master of Arts in International Affairs with a concentration in Peace and Conflict Studies. I quickly discovered my greatest interest and intellectual passion was to help humanity find their way back to an essential truth that despite cultural, religious, and economic status, we are all the same within. We have literally lived each other's lives thousands of times over in previous lives[8]. When we attack a group of people or individuals because of race, color, creed, sexuality or gender, we traumatize ourselves. We are the same as each other, with the same emotional, physical, psychological, and spiritual needs. How could I help the world regain this lost knowledge and apply it in our everyday and global lives?

In 1998, I began spending more time with my ex. We were close friends. He had become much more conservative and traditional in his religious views and was attending

---

8   Reincarnation is a natural state of our soul growth. Our soul will choose to be reborn into a new physical life, depending on the lessons it requires to move forward towards re-unification with Source/God.

Latin mass at various Catholic churches in town. I went with him at times, and other times went on my own. For me, church had always been about inspiring music, family, and belonging. I had always searched for a spiritual community that felt like home. This community seemed like an opportunity to rediscover that. Books I had been reading like the "*Conversations with God*" series by Neale Donald Walsch, "*Science of Mind*" by Ernest Holmes, and "*A Course in Miracles*" became impossible to follow. I stopped journaling and automatic writing. I had grown weary of the unchanging spiritual messages I had been receiving for years ... 'I was here for a special purpose,' 'I would author an important book,' that 'I was special.' I didn't feel special. I was very lonely on this spiritual trek. There was absolutely no one who I could identify with, except a few online friends in a spiritual network.

A painful struggle was happening within me. I came to a weighty decision: trust in my true Self, in my intuition, and continue this solitary path, or let go of it all and completely give over to the traditions of pre-Vatican II Catholicism, to being accepted and belonging, to finding affinity and love with my ex. I wish I could say I stayed true to myself, but loneliness is a strong motivator. I had a powerful subconscious program running through me, a belief that I was unworthy of unconditional love and acceptance. The instinctual need to not be alone defeated all other aspirations. I had little faith I would meet someone who would value all parts of me.   Mark proposed to me in December of 1999. From the outside it seemed sudden, but for us it was overdue. I genuinely loved him, and knew our paths were formed together from the first moment we met, if not before. We had chosen each other before birth, to work out our soul lessons together, and to be a mirror when needed. I know that he grounds me completely, which "having my head in the clouds," I needed.

When I said "I do" to him, I ignorantly said no to my awakening process. My new husband called anything metaphysical or spiritually minded, 'from the devil.' I wish I had the courage to stay true to my budding spiritual beliefs, but my need to be loved outweighed everything else then. (At this time, I did not realize the Path my soul was on, but my soul recognized the catalysts he would provide on my soul journey.) My new husband wanted a more traditional Catholic life. I convinced myself Latin mass, with its religious ceremony, meditative prayer and three note chants were preferable to the progressive, folk singing, service-oriented church community I grew up in. I joined the choir and made a home for myself there. I hoped to make friends with the women of the parish which didn't really happen. I thought once I had children, I would make connections. After two boys, I still did not feel the connection I was hoping for. The parishioners were nice, but not overly friendly.   The spiritual family I'd been hoping for never materialized in that space.

In despair, I let go of everything I used to define myself: my writing, my joyful singing, my intuitive voice, and my master's degree (discussed in a later chapter). I stopped communicating with my spiritual guides (not realizing they didn't stop communicating with me). This was perhaps the worst thing for me. A growing anger built inside of me, which blossomed into rage. This rage overwhelmed me at times, coming at me unexpectedly, leaving me shaken and spent. I had to leave the house often, so as not to take it out on my husband and little children. Years and years of repressed anger surged through me. It was as if all the anger I'd suppressed through my childhood and young adulthood had suddenly slipped its moors and would come flying out at unexpected times. The anger felt bigger than the situation most of the time. I was at a loss as to its cause, and how to manage it. I had completely forgotten about my empathic abilities. I forgot that I was a sponge and absorbed others' emotions, mistaking them for mine. I believe this occurred often. I connected with feelings of anger because of the situation at home, or my stress, and so would personalize those big feelings. I know it wasn't all mine. When I was growing up, it felt like an unspoken rule that anger was not allowed to be expressed. At least not by me. I was completely out of touch with anger. I knew there was a problem when, at age 27, I couldn't express grief at the funeral of my favorite grandpa. The excessive anger had another source which I didn't discover for many years, until my early forties.

When we suppress our emotions, we suppress them all. I couldn't feel deep sadness, fear, or even unconditional love from others. I built a wall around my heart for protection, but it ended up being my prison. Along with awareness of my emotional disconnection, was the growing realization I could no longer attend Latin mass. Everything felt so wrong to me. My heart was not in the music. The rigid and judgmental homilies left me cold; the community was very cliquish and not very welcoming. I never felt like I could share what I was thinking and feeling about spirituality and be accepted. My husband liked to be in his own prayer world, separate from me, during mass. This was painful to bear each Sunday. I couldn't find myself anywhere. Over time, the rules and regulations by which the Latin mass moved seemed ridiculous to me. Even though I had turned my back on it, my inner self was screaming at me.... This is not you!

Denying our true selves over a prolonged period, and suppressing our truth and voice, can make us physically ill. I began having stomach ailments. I experienced tremendous stress trying to hold back outbursts of rage, keeping my husband and sons happy, and pretending to be someone I'm not. In early 2007, I had a sudden excruciating abdominal attack which resulted in surgical removal of my gallbladder two months later. I later learned the spiritual cause of pain in the gallbladder is suppressed aggression and blockage of energy. Cancers can be developed from anger and rage that is not expressed and healed. My body was weakening with pain and other mysterious ailments doctors could never diagnose properly.

If I'm honest with myself, I knew I had made a mistake becoming a traditional Catholic, suppressing my inner truth and intuition for safety and security. I wanted the same beautiful connection of faith with my husband and family, my parents had. My parents loved God and each other, and it showed in everything they did with each other, and with us. I wanted that so much. Sadly, I realized the mistake I had made. I tried to ignore it, but my soul had other ideas. If I continued the path of denial, I'd likely become cancerous and even die.

Free will is not some airy-fairy concept. It is the basis for our life on earth. We came to earth knowing we would have amnesia of our true Home, in Heaven/Oneness with all. God gave us the gift of free will, so we could learn, grow, experience, and share of ourselves. We are here to remember who we truly are, to live our life's purpose with passion and love, to be of service, and to practice our true nature in every moment. We are constantly given opportunities to move closer to our soul path, or to move away. Even when we move away, there are lessons for us there. No experience is wasted for our soul. What we call evil or darkness, is an opportunity for growth. Without darkness, we cannot know light. Without fear and hatred, we cannot know love and forgiveness. Without pain and illness, we cannot know the gifts of healing. We must each go through cycles of learning. Sometimes we need more than one lesson, and the experience is repeated in a different way. I've often observed people I know go through the same hard lesson over and over. Sometimes it's relationship issues, and they keep picking the guy/gal that gives them the same lesson they ran from in a past relationship. Sometimes it's a working environment, a career choice, financial decisions, or a painful family relationship. It takes as long as it takes, and then we heal it and move on. If we choose to ignore the pain, it will eat us up from the inside. People often choose to slowly kill themselves with drugs, alcohol, food, work and lifestyle rather than face, accept, and work on healing emotional, psychological, and spiritual damage caused by past trauma.

I was grieving my childhood, my young adulthood, my expectations of what my life would be when I grew up, the dreams I had of married life, the security of a known future... and it was one of the hardest things I had experienced up to that point.

Soul to the World

4   SPIRITUAL INTERVENTION

Even though I had stopped automatic writing with my guides in the early years of my marriage, I continued inner dialogue with them. I had always "spoken" to Source and my guides my whole life. Prayer has always been interactive for me. I sang praise to God or talked with God in my mind. I continued this after 'converting' to traditional Catholicism in my late twenty's. In 2005, my spiritual guides became more assertive. They wanted me to trust what my intuition was telling me. My intuition was firmly telling me that formal religion was not the way for me. I was being 'told' to go within...that all my answers were there, waiting. It took me two years to finally accept the truth and find courage to leave the Church. It was not easy. My marriage suffered a big hit. My husband could not understand, nor did he have compassion for my decision. He considered it a direct attack on him, his beliefs, and his dreams of our life together. I was letting go of my own dreams as well. My heart was broken for everything I thought I wanted. It was so scary and hard to trust a net would appear for me. My health was deteriorating, so I knew it was time to take a leap into the unknown. I finally reached a point where anything had to be better than the emotional and physical distress, I felt every day. I had to trust it would get better. It took a willingness for self-discovery, deep inner-child healing work, acceptance of who I am and am not, and a willingness to move forward even though everything outside of myself (friends, family, husband) were telling me to please go back!

As I worried over whether I should trust my inner heart, I decided to use automatic writing again. I knew it was communication and guidance from my spiritual guides. I always made sure to protect myself, grounding to the center of the Earth, and aligning myself with Source. The following are excerpts of messages I received and wish to share with you. They hold importance for all of us.

Auriel[9] (Uriel)

What is your name?

Auriel. God has plans for you, for all of you. I am your inner voice, always here.

Who is my Real Self?

She serves others, her family, herself. She believes in others, her family, herself. She understands her destiny, her path,

---

9   Auriel is the angel of wisdom and truth, shining the light of God's truth in the darkness of confusion. His name means "God is my light" or "Fire of God" and is one of the Four Great Archangels and one of the Seven Archangels. Also known as the "Angel of Presence" and "Patron of Prophecy". (www.christianity.com)

her life. She affirms others, her family, herself. She realizes her importance to others, her family, herself. She exists here, now for them, for her.

What am I afraid of?

Betrayal, loss, loneliness to name a few. They are an illusion. You are stronger than you think. (Root fear is) Loss of your family and yourself.

Where is my anger coming from?

Anger at your fear, where you find yourself (between a rock and hard place). You become more miserable the longer you push aside your Purpose. It is your choice, your decision, but your soul knows it's Purpose. You need to forgive the sources of anger within you before it can completely leave you.

Where is this coming from?

Within/without. We are One, you and I. We. God. Humanity. We all exist together, One mind, One heart. Believe in your true purpose for being here. It will guide you. To know yourself, to teach others to know themselves, to lead, to teach, to guide, to unite.

Abraham[10] (2007)

Who is with me now?

You are truly with yourself now, and I (Abraham) am

---

10   The disincarnate Light Beings famously channeled by public speaker and best-selling author, Esther Hicks (*Ask and It Is Given*).

always here with you. When you know our name, you realize that many of us are always with you. Believe it, it is beheld by many. You will be a light for many. Your light will shine before all.

That sounds blasphemous.

No. Maybe you have heard it before because it is your Way. God believes in you. You are the light.

How can I be Light when I feel so out of control in my own life?

You are reacting to what is coming.

What is?

You are. You are going to lead many towards the light within themselves. You were chosen specifically for this life because of who you really are and have been before. You are a salvation to many.

By writing a book?

Yes. We are so pleased that you are becoming more aware of yourself and your journey on this planet is continuing. You are in the process of shifting your awareness.

Why is my body trembling?

You are sensing your arrival and the state of being a Lightbringer.

(I started feeling a pressure within myself...and a

buildup of excitement). What am I feeling?

Your angels are speaking through you. There are many and they are eager for you to become who you are meant to be. You can prepare by praying for others, meditating, and thinking of your Light.

Why can't I find a faith community that I feel comfortable with, will I ever find one?

God is listening to you always, Jenny. Be ever mindful that you will continue meeting those of same mind. You are creating your community now around you. You are all around us and we are around you. You are full of Heaven's angels, singing for you.

At this point, I was so filled with euphoria and bliss, I could barely form a thought. Intense expressions of Love, Peace, Joy, Awareness filled my whole self. Confirmation of feelings I'd felt but doubted for so long. I felt like I was going to explode into light and did not understand how my snoring husband next to me could not sense it.

Did my children choose me as their mother and why?

So, they could become who they are meant to be. You will give birth to a beautiful perfect girl in one year (prediction; my beautiful red-headed daughter was born one year later, in August 2008!) *Love is strong within you for your children. Your anger is waning and soon will extinguish as you continue your spiritual journey.*

I was experiencing a lot of fear and resistance to

making a huge change in my life.

When you look within you, you can feel Gods' Presence within you. You can access the All Knowing that is within you.

Here...I ask about demons. These are low vibration entities. They are not tied to religion, but often choose to express through it, to feed from our terror and pain.

Source

God, I need to talk to you. I have been reading *Conversations with God* by Neale Donald Walsch. I am confused. What about Satan/Devil? Miracles and Apparitions? Saints like Padre Pio, Exorcisms... please explain.

It began in the hearts of Man. A knowing that we are all One. And then, it changed, the knowing. "Adam & Eve" ...fear began. Fear of loss at first, then fear of God. I became something to fear. Life happens, and people need explanations. The proverbial "Why"? You seek to know Me fully. You can know Me only so far, at present. To know Me as you wish, you must take chances and risks. Believing despite what you hear and see. Are you ready to do that?

Yes, I am.

Why did Padre Pio experience torture from demons?

He asked to be. He needed to have a belief, such that he needed constant reminders of who he really was, so he could help the masses of people more fully. He could bear the pain, so that others didn't. The demons were disciples who took a wrong turn.

They were manifestations of those who wished ill of Padre Pio, who didn't want his good works and his healing in the world. They feared Pio and his message of forgiveness and love.

What are Possessions?

Possessions are of the Soul. When a soul is defeated or lost, or suffering even unbeknownst to the physical self, then evilness manifests through them. They become a harbor for evil and fear, of the world. The possessed chose to be tested in this way before they were born.

What are demons?

There are various levels of being for (all) Spirit. Demons are the lowest form. They are always evolving. But demons are not human and have never lived a human life, nor will they. They are not from Hell, as there is truly no such place, but they do tend to spend their time on lower levels of the spiritual plane, or on other dimensions for that matter.

Why are they allowed to exist if they cause so much harm, and don't seem to have a sense of anything but harm?

All God's creatures both great and small, correct.

They can't be considered God's creatures.

They were created for a purpose, through desires of others, they were created. They exist.

Is there a Hell with torments?

No, there is not a physical place. Many believe in it, and it helps guide them towards a better life lived, but there is not really a Hell, unless that is what they expect or believe they deserve. Hell is an expression of our spirit's lack of belief in itself. Trust in what your heart tells you.

Why did Yeshua (Jesus) reference it?

Because he spoke to the belief of the times. He made us realize that there was a place that speaks to the minds of men and that we called Hell... But truly, such a place doesn't exist. Believe in what your heart tells you.

Why did Yeshua die on the cross?

He died in order that we be made whole once more, whole in Spirit.

Why do so many people believe in Satan/The Devil?

Satan is not real except in the minds of Men. I tell you this, Satan lives only in the hearts of men and women who live in fear and hatred of themselves. That fear and hatred can (physically) manifest, even into the seeming innocent (possessions). The guises are all created and made manifest. Satan is the embodiment of fear and hatred in the world. It is Man's way of coping with fear of death and eternity. Belief of the devil has been genetically encoded, it seems, the way it continues. Lucifer is not evil or dark. Lucifer is Light to those who are lost. There is evil in the world, and in other worlds there are beings called demons and other beings who wish to do harm to others for the sheer pleasure of it. The power they think they gain. It will take them a long time to evolve from this state. Eventually they will... (In the Law of One[11], they are referred to as 'Service to Self' entities.)

So, evil acts and deeds, they are motivated by individuals' hatred and fear of themselves? It is our choice on how we react or not.

Yes.

Apparitions of holy figures from the past serve as reminders of where we come from and who we really are.

You recognize them. They come from your True Home. They offer hope in a world that seems to offer none. People desperately seek reattachment to their soul's Home. Apparitions serve as reminders. Healing occurs when their Soul remembers.

I am always with you Jenny. You are one of My Messengers. You recognize the Call.

Metatron[12]

On Anger

You need to be at peace in your heart. You achieve that peace by consciously choosing to feel peace. You can choose it by letting yourself watch nature in action or listening to soothing music and/or other forms of expression. Make a conscious decision

---

11   Law of One are a set of books created through channeling the 6th Density civilization of RA in 1980-81, published from 1982-1984 and 1998. More information later in the book and in Bibliography.

12   Archangel Metatron is the Archangel of Empowerment. Is one of only two angels believed to have ascended from a human incarnation (Enoch) into the angelic realm. Metatron is also known as keeper of the Akashic Records.

to choose peace and the anger will leave you.

On Doubt and Fear

You must push forward through doubts and fear because it is perception, not reality. You create your own reality. What do you choose? Fear or Love? Peace or Unhappiness? Money or lack? You choose it all. You doubt and fear because in your heart, you wonder if you are fully worthy. You are! Do not doubt it any longer. I am here to tell you; you are more worthy than you realize.

When you are ready, we will make you aware of your true Purpose. Your true purpose on Earth will help to change how people think about their world and place in it.

Now is the time for a rising of consciousness. The time grows near when critical mass will occur, and most will understand. The 'others' are pushing at the knowing, with fear, through terroristic acts, through anger, through mayhem and murder, trying to push aside what their soul is trying to tell them. It may get crazy before it gets any better. Push on through, we will guide you, as you guide yourself, as you made the intention to do so from the beginning.

Who speaks?

I am Metatron. Humans create names/labels, there are no names/labels in Spiritual Realms)

There is so much more to life than living, breathing and being. It is within all of you to know the great hope of your Soul. Are you courageous enough to reach out for it? To grasp it and know it is so? Do so. Do not wait for a trumpet out of the sky, it won't come to you that way. It is a whisper, a dream, a seeking wish that pulls and draws at you. Explore it, nurture it and it will lead you into worlds you have barely imagined. My words flow through your pen quickly because I am so eager for you to hear and understand your Purpose, your passion. You have always sensed (that) you are here for a bigger purpose.

Another bout of frustration about feeling stuck and not moving forward.

Will I ever get out of my own way? (as expressed to me by Abraham, when I met them at a conference with Spiritual Channeler, Esther Hicks)

You can. You must be willing to let go of Ego. You must be willing to let go to God. Trust in Him/Us/Yourself. That is what is required. You've known it for a long time. It is what you fear most, letting go of control. Loss of control is so very scary for humanity. You control, pull in tighter, those you fear losing, and yet you lose the very part of yourself you seek. Don't you see?

How do I let go?

Breathe through it. When you feel the tentacles of control slipping around you, cut them. The river flows without someone making it flow. The flower grows, the birds fly, you live. Who controls you?

What keeps me in place, unable to move forward?

Fear. Fear and lack of understanding of who you truly are. Unwillingness to take the leap of faith. Imagine yourself standing on the edge of a cliff, with only the promise of a net to appear. Can you (jump)?

Often, I feel so distant from where I want to be, who I want to be...selfishness, fear, etc.

You allow fear to rule you often. Allowing fear to rule you means you don't have to take any risks for yourself. You can just stay the way things are and forget about your own wishes. But you want more than that for yourself. You want love and peace and financial wealth, and freedom for your family and yourself. To get those things, you must be willing to let go of the fear, push through it and move forward. What do you choose? Fear or Love? Peace or unhappiness? Money or lack of? You choose it all. You have doubts and fear because in your heart, you are wondering if you are fully worthy. You ARE! Do not doubt it any longer. I AM HERE to tell you that you are more worthy than you realize.

I think the trouble I have, is that I Do know that all I want is there for me. I need to believe I Deserve it!

That is correct. Once you believe and know you are deserving of happiness, then it will all be yours.

So, how do I get to that place?

Pray, meditate, think upon it. Think of why you believe you are not worthy. Get to the heart of that. Look at your childhood.

(Clear ancient programs.)

When you are ready, we will make you aware of your true Purpose. Your true purpose on Earth is one where you will be giving much to others and helping to change how people think about their world and their place in it.

This is the first time my True Purpose is referenced in spiritual communication with me.

> *I am all that is.*
> *I come through you,*
> *the self, the outer self that is not you, but is only self.*
> *You/I*
> *We are one.*
> *Allow the I to feel the Self,*
> *Allow the I to feel the self,*
> *Feel the emotions. Let it pass.*
> *It flows; be one with it.*
> *I am expression, I am purpose.*
> *I am life that flows.*
> *Within each soul,*
> *Within each life that lives on our planet,*
> *And so many others within and without your universe.*
> *'You' that are aware of the I, are present with us now.*
> *Are always present.*
> *Let the self, who feels the rage or pain, continue its way.*
> *We are one, always with you.*

Why haven't I allowed myself to be successful?

FEAR, it always comes down to that, doesn't it? Fear of success; fear of failure not so much...that is your ego leading you away from any changes it may encounter. With success comes change in your life, to your way of living, to your way of believing about yourself and your own goals, reaching them, achieving them will do so much towards enriching your own soul.

Only fear holds you back at this point. Fear is manifesting as boredom, annoyance, irritation, fatigue, overeating to distraction, tv and movies, books, everything, and anything except what you really want to do, which is get going. So just decide to do it and start.

Create time for yourself. You are worth every moment you give to yourself, because ultimately you are giving it to others. God is pleased with you; with the progress you've made and for where you are continuing to grow towards. Trust Him, even if you do not trust yourself.

Higher Self, Metatron, Abraham, Yeshua, Source...

Who speaks to me now?

We are those who dream for you. Abraham or teachers, or angels, or God, or higher self, we go by all those names and more.

It feels like life is running amok and I'm not manifesting my thoughts...or am I? Who is here with me now? I need counsel...

I am (known as) Metatron. I am Many.

Now is not the time for counsel, but for making a new purpose and letting your dreams fulfill themselves. You are feeling the lack of it in your life, and it is causing you injury and pain emotionally and physically. You must move forward Jenny, in your dreams. Your Spirit seeks to know itself through the creation of its essence. Which you know, is given in written word. When you finally begin writing again, you will feel the fulfillment you have been seeking. A story yearns to be unfolded within you and you yearn with aching longing to give voice to this story. It tempts and teases you, pulling you ever forward until you must lift pen to paper as you are doing now and dive into the creative flow, becoming all that is for you to seek to become and all that you are.

You have always sensed how you will live far more than you are living now. Yes, it is true, your answer lives within (the) asking for it. When you allow yourself to pursue your dreaming, all your wishes will come to fruition. It is waiting for you.

Joy is the essence of your and everyone's Higher Self. You are attempting to reconnect to that aspect of yourself. You will and do from time to time. We will help you to achieve it (with more ease). Be aware of your communication with us. Take time to connect.

Let your heart take you to where it is yearning to go. Do not concern yourself with other's opinions. They only keep you from observing and acting upon your observations. Maybe you are ready to begin writing your story.

What is our similar goal?

To bring knowledge to many. To heal the masses. To bring hope. To bring love. To give what is needed and necessary. To be what you are intended for, a hope for many.

How many are you?

More than enough. We are so numerous; you could not truly list them. You only need to know we are here to serve you.

What kind of higher-level guides are you?

Angel's and other beings such as disincarnate entities and Beings of Light.

Any names they are known by, that I would recognize? (we humans have such a need to label!)

Yes, you would recognize the name of Jesus, Paul, and Mary (yes) and Isaac and messengers of light like Metatron.

I have begun thinking again about what I am meant to write. I come again to the idea of a soul's journey.... mine, perhaps...

Yes, that is the way for you. To write of your own journey, to tell the story, as you have experienced it, and to allow others to know of it. So many others have been waiting for a voice to give a name to the experience they know of but cannot name. You have named it. It is here, to be found, through you, to be written.

Why am I afraid?

Because it is a dream that can be realized. A path that is to be followed and it is there for you, if only you can reach out for it. It requires you to believe in yourself. To believe that you are all that we have said...and so much more. You must BELIEVE it. When you believe it, you Know it...you live it. You are coming to Believe it, and then to Know it, Jenny. Trust us. Yourself. Anything that comes from your heart and knowing, cannot be wrong.

To write the journey of my soul...touching upon the incidences of my life, which have molded me to become the person I am...who I chose to be in the Before. The choices I made to continue to allow difficulty, knowing, intuitively, that it was for a specific reason. Some would call it Karma, or other things. Preparation for a life to be lived. Later choices made...out of fear (of being lonely, of not finding love) ... choices that lead to a new path...perhaps a more difficult path than was needed...or perhaps the path I was meant to take.

It would take eleven years before I started the writing process of my book. I had so many fears and doubts to overcome, as well as so much self-healing to undergo. Here, I express my frustration...

WILL I EVER GET OUT OF MY OWN WAY?

You can. You must be willing to let go of self. You must be willing to let go to God, and what that means fully. Trust in Him, Us and Yourself. That is what is required. You've known it for a long time.

HOW DO I LET GO?

I know you wish so much to be able to let go...allow yourself Jenny. You will feel happiness again. You will know peace. Your creativity will be unbound and will flow once more for you.

Your children are growing, and they will thrive without your hovering. You need to let them unfurl their own wings, so that they may learn to fly on their own. They will always come back to you, never fear. You are "Mommy" to them. You can never lose them.

WHY HAVENT I BEEN ABLE TO MOVE FORWARD ALL THIS TIME?

FEAR. And lack of understanding of who you really are, and unwillingness to take that leap. Imagine yourself standing on the edge of the cliff, with only the promise of a net to maybe appear... can you, do it?

To be free is what it is all about. This life and the lessons to be learned here. Your soul longs to be free, to be able to join once more with all. That is the true trick to life and to live...to be free, you must be willing to let go of life and living. (A song's refrain just went past...'to be willing to surrender...')

2009

Where does my anger stem?

From many sources. Some are from your childhood, some from your parents, some from your sister, some from your spouse, some from within yourself. But overall, a lifetime of suppressing anger has created this overflow that has created a great disturbance in your life. It is time to change it, to heal it, release it, and let it all go completely. You need to forgive the sources of anger within you before it completely leaves you.

How do I begin to forgive? Is there a ritual, do I need to talk this out...can I do it alone?

Yes, you can do those things, but alone works just as well, as we are all connected, and they will hear you on a spiritual plane.

Am I being attacked from a spiritual source...a malignant one? (I identify it in 2010)

You can feel it sometimes. This depression is from the anger and suppressed emotion you feel, it is also from a source outside of yourself, this source you call malignant, is not of this earth. It is from a different place, and it has attached itself to you because you have so much life force flowing within you, and you are such a beacon of light for so many. It seeks the warmth you give out. It wants it for itself, and so tries to suck it from you.

How can I get rid of it?

By doing the above, and by truly forgiving yourself of every role you have played in your own pain and fearfulness. It feeds off the fear within you. Once this is done, it will leave you.

Does this badness have a name?

Demons don't usually have names.

There is a demon attracted to me?

That is the name you as humans have given to them. They do not come from your planet. They are lower creatures, and suck at life force energy. You are extraordinarily strong, and so you have attracted one to you.

Would a healing from an outside source be helpful?

It may, but most of the healing must come from within yourself, for any outside healing to work. You must want it enough. It is attracted to stress and fear and anxiety within you and shows up during those times. (Your Guides) have been working hard for you to reach this understanding. We are grateful that you understand and can hear us. Perhaps it will help you now.

Source (2010)

What is it God...what am I feeling?

You seek knowledge that has been living within you for some time Jenny. The sole reason you have been seeking it outside of yourself is because of fear and doubt and the dis-ability to believe you have this power within yourself already. You only need to believe truly that you have this power, and you will have it.

How do I do this...believe this completely and unconditionally?

Just so. The only way to believe in yourself is to do so. Sit down with yourself and realize that you and only you have ever had the capacity to create the life you dream of. It is a mental thing that you have. Something created long ago, (Program) perhaps to strengthen you for challenging times, but which is no longer needed. You need to drop this shield you have drawn around yourself. You can use prayer, mantra, meditation, visualization, but you need to cut away the shroud that keeps you in place and cut off from your abilities. Visualize yourself cutting through the grayness, the darkness, shining a light through the fog, blowing it away, revealing clarity, wisdom and understanding. Believe in yourself, and your gifts. Your gifts of wisdom, truth, honesty, love, creation, heart, dreams, belief in others.

I had no idea I was being mentally and spiritually prepared for a momentous event that would completely alter the trajectory of my life to that point. As I was told by a medical intuitive later, my soul is on a sped-up journey and had built two lives into one. In the upcoming chapter, I "died" to my old self, and was re-born into a completely new and unknown Self.

Soul to the World

5 GENERATIONAL DARKNESS

"When moments of fear come, be fearful, tremble with fear. Fear comes, it is natural. When you allow fear and you tremble, watch it, enjoy it, and in that watching you will transcend it" – Osho[13]

I will speak of a secret that has been hidden from conscious awareness for millennia. It has toppled nations, and broken societies, relationships and families beyond repair. It is something we are genetically programmed over the years to forget, so we may live out our lives somewhat happily, even if in ignorance of the truth. These secrets underlie all our darkest fairytales. We must relegate barely remembered horror into mythology and fantasy, to survive. The darkest deeds of humanity including witch hunts and burnings, inquisitions, indigenous genocides, murderous feuds, and every form of slavery and war can be laid at its doorstep. In modern times, the effects of this secret have begun to

---

13   Osho, The Nature of Fear: Fear Is Nothing But Absence of Love, on Audible, March 22, 2016

surface. It is a darkness that resides in the deepest part of the psyche. It is the root cause of the sexual slave trade, rise of violence amidst our youth, and deep-seated hatreds which cause people in power to do evil things in the name of religion, politics, and power. Its tools are excessive addiction to alcohol, sex, power, drugs, and violence. It abides in ignorance, contempt, apathy, hatred, bigotry, racism and sexism, indifference, prejudice, fear, shame, and spiritual weakness.

I became aware of this secret suddenly at age 40, after the most frightening and shocking experience of my life.

It happened one night...

I charged violently awake, gasping for air around a closed off throat. My husband murmured in his sleep and rolled away from me. I sat up clutching my chest, feeling my heart beating hard and fast. A dream floated on the edge of unconscious memory.... gone. I glanced at the clock, 2:30 am. I lay back down and tried to sleep but instead felt a spike of anxiety. Like many Empaths, I'd had anxiety my whole life but had learned to manage it on my own. I started going through the steps...talking to myself rationally, taking slow deep breaths, repeating a calming mantra..." Christ within me, Christ all around me." Rather than helping, the irrational fear grew in intensity.

I got up and began pacing around the room, rubbing

my chest. 'I'm fine, everything is fine... there is nothing to fear. I am safe.' I glanced down at my husband and thought about waking him. This feeling wasn't getting better, only worse. This was not like my previous anxiety attacks. I ran into the bathroom and splashed my face with water, drinking some out of the tap. Worse, so much worse.... I went to my bed and reached out to my husband.

"Mark!" He woke suddenly and said in alarm "What?! Are you ok?" He got out of bed and came over to me when he saw my strained white face. I was gasping and struggling to remain upright. Weak and dizzy, I put my arms around his neck and leaned onto him. "I don't know what I'm feeling.... intense pressure, fear.... I, I .... can't...." At this point, I lost all sensation of hearing, touch, sight, and body awareness. It felt like I was being sucked down into an impenetrable black void with no escape.

I was falling into a gaping abyss. The blackness was unrelenting all around me. As I free fell, I felt the most intense fear I've ever experienced in my life. There were no words. This fear was outside of reasoning, outside of belief. All the fear of the world pressing in on me, down into me, trying to take my life. And it got worse. For a long while, I was completely focused on a single point. I felt like I would faint, I begged God....' please, God, please.... take me. I can't do this anymore.... Why?' Ragged faint words came out of me, disjointed, nonsensical... "I'm sorry....

please...please...I'll be good...don't leave! Please.... I'm sorry, I'm so sorry...." The Desolation and Fear...was so oppressive, I didn't understand how I was still breathing, still alive. I did have a sense of me.... but nothing else.

Slowly, I began to come back to myself. My breathing began to slow its race, I felt my body and my husband's arms around me, holding me tightly. I heard him asking urgently "Jenny, are you ok? Jenny! Do I call 911?"

In that oppressive space, there was no time. It was timeless, forever. I was Orpheus descending into hell. My mind skittered away from the memory. I glanced at the clock, 3:30 am. My breathing began to calm, and I was able, finally, to speak. In a shaking voice, I tried to tell him what happened. I gave up when I started to spike anxiety again. I asked him to call 911. My rational mind was trying to make sense of it. Did I have a heart attack? I was only forty and there was no heart history in my immediate family. I'd had heart arrythmia during my life, but nothing serious. My breathing was erratic. The paramedics took my measurements. They determined an event had occurred, although they weren't sure of the cause. I went to the hospital in an ambulance, so my husband could stay home with our three small children. After much testing, the doctor determined I'd had a severe panic attack and prescribed medication I gratefully took. I was still shaking from my experience hours later.

My husband came with our 20-month-old daughter to pick me up that morning. I had no explanation for him, or for myself. Any explanation I'd tried to give would sound irrational. Nothing like this had ever happened to me.

I tried to go about my normal day. In quiet moments, my horrific memories came rushing back. I began breathing fast and felt anxiety. That night, and every night for three months, I relived the experience with different variations. I couldn't wrap my mind around what was happening to me or why. If I thought about it at all, the anxiety kicked in. Each night, around 2-3 am, I would wake suddenly to a feeling of doom. My body would start vibrating violently, starting with my lower legs, moving up to my trunk, my arms, my shoulders, my chest. At this point, I would feel pressure and start burping. When it got to my throat, the anxiety tightened everything. I tried breathing slowly, going through all the tools I'd learned. It didn't really help. I spent around 40 min to an hour fighting hard not to slip back into the abyss. Eventually, the feeling would start to fade, and exhaustion would take over and allow me to sleep.

After two months of this, I realized I needed emotional and therapeutic support. It took two months before I could begin to describe what I was feeling without going into hysterics. An incredible Family Constellation therapist (and family friend) told me that whenever the nighttime anxiety showed up, to call her, no matter the time. I felt so much better knowing someone was with me in that bottomless pit. She didn't call me crazy, just listened with compassion and unconditional love. Because of her, I was able to come to a place where I could attempt to identify my experience. She encouraged me to write a journal during the day. I did so, asking what it was and why it happened. A horrible image appeared in my mind, and I drew it. A monstrous face peered out at me from the page. It was a huge gaping maw with rows and rows of razor-sharp teeth that spun around in feverish movement. It fed from my fear. It was Fear. I shared this with my therapist. She asked if this entity had said anything to me? I said no, but that during the first night strange words had come out of my mouth that I didn't understand. I shared them with her. She didn't seem surprised and told me I was being attacked by an evil entity and she could help me when I was ready.

It took another month of re-experiencing the malevolent fear entity before I had the strength for confrontation. One night, as my body tightened in anxiety and its vibration routine started, I decided, enough was enough! It was time to confront the entity and end it. I called Source and my spiritual guides to me, and consciously stepped back into the oppressively dark chasm. The malevolent Being was in front of me. I only saw its gnashing sharp teeth and felt its evil intent. Suddenly, a powerful Light Being stood next to me. It was tall, incandescent in white gold, and held a bright glowing sword. My consciousness entered the Light Being. We brought the sword down on the entity, destroying it. It felt final. The abyss disappeared, but the Light Being stayed within me. From time to time, I can feel its power stretch out from me. I envision wings although I know that is a human construct. I know this evil entity has been harming my maternal family line all the way back to its ancient origin. I stopped the monster in its tracks. Not only stopped, but healed soul trauma through all our generations.

I asked God everyday why this happened to me. Why has it continued to affect me so strongly? Until this experience, I'd lived a mostly normal life. The infrequent supernatural experiences could be chalked up to having extra-sensory perception, which is common in some families. Spooky ghost stories to share with friends. This experience turned everything I thought I knew on its head. I could not rationalize what happened to me or explain my absolute knowledge of divine intervention. My old life passed away, and I was reborn into spiritual truth, knowledge and understanding. There could be no going back, only forward on my spiritual path. I was no longer afraid of death.

After an intensive three years of healing (which I share in the following chapters), I understood why I had this experience. I came to help bring awareness to the world of the Truth. Evil exists. Low level entities we call demons exist. They are physically manifested into this world through evil/dark thoughts and actions of lost souls. These creatures are not of this world, at the lowest vibration, and feed on fear, terror, pain, rage, and chaos. They create or expand upon negative situations/feelings amongst individuals, relationships, family systems and large groups of people to maximize as much fear and hatred as possible. They have been doing this for as long as humanity has held consciousness awareness. Low vibrational/demonic influence separates us from our Truth...that we are one with Source and powerful creators on our own.

When the first humans were created, they were given a gift... the power to create anything they so desired. Power can be used for good or for evil, it is always a choice as illustrated in the religious story of Adam and Eve. In male dominated cultures, Eve was blamed for the Fall because of her feminine nature. I believe women have been attacked and vilified through history for their intuitive and healing gifts, their ability to create life, and their closeness with Source. Low vibrational entities were able to influence those filled with jealousy, fear, rage, and shame. The darkness that resided within their hearts drove a purposed wedge between them and Source. From that time forward these negative entities controlled the spiritually weak within families and societies, creating situational horror, terror, and abject misery. True evil exists. Its creation may not be religious in nature, but a result of repressed negative emotion.

I believe ongoing evil thoughts and resulting actions, when not surrendered and let go, can eventually manifest physically into the world through creation of low vibrational entities[14]. The purpose of their physical manifestation is to be seen, cleared and healed. Their existence misunderstood through time, low vibrational entities (demons) have been passed down through families and institutions since humanity first became conscious. We associate demons

---

14   Evil low vibrational entities can also manifest through intentions of satanists and the dark occult.

with religion as they are spoken of in the Old Testament and other ancient religious texts. What if they were created by us? What would happen if instead of reacting with extreme fear or suppression, we faced the entity with courage and collaborated with a high vibrational therapist or healer to permanently clear it. What would society be like? The peace we have longed for can be ours if we make it happen.

***

By mutual choice, before birth, I made a spiritual contract with a powerful lightworker, healer and member of my Soul Tribe[15]. This person chose to be born into a family with an ancient malevolent entity that had been conducting every form of evil abuse and torture through the spiritually weakest family members for millennia. It received the most power and control when it could successfully corrupt the source of unconditional love (parents). We both made this choice consciously, knowing our lives would be difficult, painful, and hard to overcome at times. As powerful Light Beings, we each took the role our Soul required of us. As lightworkers, we understood the profound healing effects which would reverberate throughout our family's future generations.

You might ask how you can help change the darkness that may reside in your own family of origin. Ask to be shown the Way. Source listens to our prayers and thoughts. It has always been our

---

15   A Soul Tribe is a group of people who chose to incarnate with you, who help support your spiritual journey, encourage you, are catalysts if needed, and are true soul friends. They often show up right before making a huge change in your life, to support your next steps.

free will, to choose which path we will take... towards light, or towards darkness. Source honors that choice. You can heal yourself, help heal your family, and potentially your generational line. Spiritual teachers and healers can provide the tools you need. You must be willing to be completely honest with yourself, to face the darkness, walk through it, and come out the other side. You must ask the tough questions and accept the answers. Therapists with family systems expertise are excellent support. With acceptance begins the process of healing. In the following chapter, I share tools I have used to heal myself and my family. I hope you might find use for them. If it resonates for you, it will work. There are those who were born for this specific purpose, and they are bringing the Light of Truth to human consciousness. The time for healing is now. I invite you to journey into your own story.

PART II
SOUL HEALING

"There is coming a time, when the light that has been shadowing you, will strengthen and shine brightly upon you, blinding you to all else but what is next for you. This light will shine so brightly, you will not be able to do aught else but listen and follow it"

~My Higher Self, September 2010

Soul to the World

6   ANXIETY

A common side effect of clairsentience[16] is anxiety. Every Empath I have ever met has struggled with anxiety off and on throughout their life. Anxiety haunts empaths in quiet solitude and cacophonic chaos. Many empaths are created from traumatic childhoods; others are born empaths. When we are unconscious of our empathic abilities, we absorb fear, worry, anxiety, and anger from others. We make them our own, or we become bombarded with intense emotions from those around us. If we haven't learned to spiritually protect and ground ourselves[17], we are in a constant state of 'fight or flight.' I was born an empath, endured childhood trauma, and experienced chronic anxiety. At the age of seven, I had a traumatic experience which left me emotionally scarred for years. My parents had safely locked my sleeping sisters

---

16   Clairsentience is the extra sensory ability to perceive emotional or psychic energy that is imperceptible to the five standard senses.
17   Dr. Judith Orloff explains clearly how to protect and ground yourself in her book *The Empaths Survival Guide, Life Strategies for Sensitive People.*

and I into a motorhome overnight, while attending a family reunion. We were watched over by a teen who left at some point. In the middle of the night, I awoke suddenly in a dark and unfamiliar environment. I felt completely alone in the darkness and was hysterical with terror. After a time, I felt my father holding, rocking, and reassuring me. It was many years before I was able to feel safe away from my family. When fear of abandonment or feeling trapped was subconsciously triggered, I felt physically sick and frozen with fear, unable to interact or engage in normal social activities.

I never attended therapy for anxiety or took medication in my youth. I learned coping mechanisms along the way like paper bag or slow count breathing. For me, the best resource to recover from uncontrollable racing thoughts was talking with someone for about ten to fifteen minutes about mundane topics and journaling. Eventually, my breathing normalized, and my thoughts calmed. As a college student, I added a mantra which came to me spiritually *"Christ within me, Christ all around me."* With regular practice, my coping mechanisms and mantra greatly reduced severe anxiety. I healed myself of anxiety and panic attacks by my mid-twenties.

Approximately ten years later during my Fear event, the real source of anxiety awakened within me. As a child and young adult, I learned how to live with anxiety without looking for its root source. In 2010, I could no longer pretend

I was fine. Free falling through the abyss, I spontaneously confronted my family's dark history. Along with awakening to my True Self, this event compelled me to address my body's growing sense of alarm. Dr. Russell Kennedy[18], bestselling author of *Anxiety Rx*, discovered alarm is the real cause of anxious discomfort within the body. Anxiety is created when we ignore the 'alarming' state of our body. To heal anxiety, we are required to leave our thought-controlled minds and egos and feel our way through our bodies. Dr. Kennedy tells us our body alarm system stems from ignoring the needs of our inner child. When our inner child's needs aren't met or are reacting to remembered childhood trauma, we must feel the origin of our inner child's pain, to let go of and heal it.

In my early to mid-twenties, I spent a lot of time working with and being present to my inner child. My mom had introduced me to the concept, as she was navigating her own healing strategies from authors like John Bradshaw[19], who coined the term 'wounded inner child" in his bestselling book *Homecoming*. Little Jenny, as I affectionately called her, had been traumatized by feelings of abandonment, long-term bullying, sadness, loneliness, and lack of fun and play. She required my attention. I healed 'her' as a young adult but forgot about her when I married and began raising

18   Russell Kennedy, M.D. wrote *Anxiety Rx: A New Prescription for Anxiety Relief from the Doctor Who Created It*
19   John Bradshaw, bestselling author of *Homecoming* and motivational speaker on topics of the wounded inner child, dysfunction in families, and codependency

my own children.

A growing sense of alarm has been generated within almost everyone in the last few decades. It is sparked by an overwhelming sense we are not safe in our bodies, our homes, our communities, our countries or on the planet. The media, political figures, celebrities, and people on social media stoke the fire with dramatic claims and questionable facts. Those with chronic anxiety are barely holding themselves together. So many of my friends and family worry all the time. They fear for themselves, for their children and elder parents' safety, they fear loss of jobs, they fear what our government is doing to take care of threats, whether environmental or human made, they fear what is being put into their food, they fear leaving their homes or talking to people. This is on top of the chronic anxiety and phobias many people live with every day. We sense we are being lied to by the media, our governments, Big Business and Big Pharma. Our intuition is working in overdrive, trying to communicate with us. Because so many still don't trust their senses, it feels like overwhelming anxiety. Anxiety to be medicated, ignored, pushed aside. Our inner children beg us to listen. They are telling us that everything is not ok.

Each one of us has the power to change our life and heal from the alarm and anxiety permanently. Recognize the truth for what it is and stop hiding from it. Listen to your inner child and respond. Re-connect with your feeling body and let go of your controlling thoughts. Stay in the present moment. What are you angry or afraid about? What are you denying and why? Why are you depressed? Delve deep. Where in your body are you feeling the distress? What are you giving up, to "keep the peace"? Identify your emotion, surrender and let it go.

Maybe you are an Empath or a Highly Sensitive Person[20] and have been absorbing the emotions of everyone around you. You don't recognize this, and so assume you are the one angry, you are the one depressed, you are the one anxious. It is often not you. Then, people are medicated for something they do not even have. There are side effects to these medications, which create a need for more medication. Overdosing and lethal mixing occur often. We wonder why there is so much fear in the world, so much anger, so much sickness and death, so much murder and mayhem. Start healing the root cause. Feel through your body, what is causing your anxiety. Where does your alarm originate? What is your inner child trying to tell you? By having the courage to look within, instead of without, we can heal ourselves, and thereby heal our world.

---

20   *The Highly Sensitive Person*, written by psychologists Elaine and Arthur Aron, who discuss and identify people with highly developed sensitivity to others pain, to beauty, and those who are overwhelmed by sensory stimuli.

Soul to the World

7   HEALING TOOLS

HOMEOPATHY

After the first few months of severe anxiety and reliving the *abyss* every night, I found a few "go to" tools that helped support my ongoing recovery process. Prescription Zoloft with an infrequent Ativan to help me through the worst moments. I always used a minimal amount, as I didn't want to become dependent, and wanted to get off the medicine as quickly as possible. I took it for approximately 10 months so I could function as a mother, a wife, and employee. I worked through the bad days by practicing skills I learned from my therapist, using EFT (see below) and continued support from my mom. Aromatherapy often helps promote healing. When physical vibrations first began, I immediately took out my Angelica essential oil and dabbed critical points, my crown, forehead, throat, heart, and ears. Breathing in the gentle scents soothed my racing heart, while I softly chanted *"Christ within me, Christ all around me."* This practice centered me completely. In time, the scent alone would calm me. If my anxiety weren't too severe, I would use lavender oil. I also took Epsom salt baths frequently and journaled daily, expressing anything that needed a voice. Through my healing, sound therapy was necessary.

I find peace, solace, and comfort in sounds of nature, meditative instrumentals, and Native American flute music. I can close my eyes and imagine myself in a forest, near mountain lakes or desert landscapes. It is very relaxing. YouTube has excellent meditation and therapeutic resources. My favorite YouTube station is *Inner Lotus Music*. Put in key words and see what pops up for you. Go with the title that resonates for you. If you head to an alternative health store, there are large selections of homeopathic tinctures for almost every health concern. It is the intent behind the use that creates healing. Experiment and find what works best for you.

EFT (Emotional Freedom Technique)

Before I recognized a need for healing, I discovered Emotional Freedom Technique. EFT was created by Gary Craig, a Stanford graduate, in 1995. It is an incredibly powerful healing technique used by hundreds of thousands worldwide. While working at UC Davis Center for Health and Aging in my early thirties, I helped organize health and wellness conferences. At one event, an EFT practitioner gave a seminar on Emotional Freedom Technique. He was eager to share the wonderful health benefits of tapping for older adults and their families. EFT works by tapping specific trigger points along our body's energy meridian. It is believed negative thoughts and beliefs cause blockages to our energy flow, causing sickness and disease. People all over the world have found tremendous relief using this method. It can be done with a practitioner, or by oneself. It is an excellent source of relief for stress and anxiety, PTSD, mental and emotional burnout, worry, fear, anger, grief, chronic pain, and so much more. There are a variety of video resources on YouTube, as well as internet articles and books. I had been feeling tremendous waves of resentment and pain surrounding my decision to leave the Catholic Church. My anger was directed mostly towards myself, with pain .and guilt at how my husband would feel. I was so upset; I made myself physically ill. I spent a month working with an EFT practitioner, tapping along meridian points every day until I found peace. I was able to get past my fear and guilt to make the right choice for my health and wellbeing. Working through the effects of the 'fear event' was still an uphill battle but having EFT as a support every day greatly helped. I have included resources at the back of this book, where you can find more information about the use of this healing tool.

HO'OPONOPONO

Ho'oponopono is a powerful ancient Hawaiian healing and problem-solving process. The prayers we know today, originated with a Hawaiian Kahuna Lapa 'au named Morrnah Nalamaku Simeona. She is the founder of modern-day Ho'oponopono and used the self-forgiveness prayer and many others to miraculously cleanse and heal an individual from anything causing emotional, mental, spiritual, or physical harm. One of her more powerful prayers is as follows, she suggests memorizing and repeating four times, but writing it down works as well.

"Spirit, Superconscious, please locate the origin of my feelings, thoughts of _____.

(Fill in the blank with your belief, feeling, or thoughts that you want to erase). *Take every level, layer, area, and aspect of my being to this origin. Analyze it and resolve it perfectly with God's truth.*

Come through all generations of time and eternity. Healing every incident and its appendages based on the origin.

Please do it according to God's will until I am at the present, filled with light and truth. God's peace and love, forgiveness of myself for my incorrect perceptions.

Forgiveness of every person, place, circumstances and events which contributed to this, these feelings, thoughts and beliefs."

I first became aware of *Ho'oponopono* after talking with my mom about unresolved and lingering emotional pain from some family members who were unable to accept me for myself. She suggested I look up Dr. Hew Len, a famous clinical psychologist who had permanently healed and cleared out a criminal psych ward filled with aggressive and dangerous inmates. The hospital was depressing and hopeless. They had a skeleton staff as employees either quit in short amounts of time or called in sick regularly. When Dr. Len was hired, he didn't appear to do much, remaining in his office going through patient files. The nursing and correctional staff figured he would last a month and then move on, as most clinical staff had. He continued to come to work each day, remaining cheerful and positive, although not meeting with patients. When the staff asked his approach, he mentioned the Ho'oponopono prayer. Over the course of four years, the inmate's dangerous aggression abated and then stopped. Working conditions improved, until they had a waiting list for employment. Most of the criminals were eventually released and the psych ward closed. He was able to heal them, by healing himself. The belief behind this prayer is that anything that happens to you, or your perception within the world, is your own creation and your own responsibility to fix. It is not about fault, but responsibility. If you perceive a problem, then it is your responsibility to repair it. This prayer and others created by Dr. Len's teacher, Kahuna Simeona, bring incredible and permanent healing to its practitioners.

In a place of acceptance, I visualized each person I felt hurt by, and repeated the mantra four times (for best effect): *"I'm sorry. Please forgive me. Thank you. I love you."* I did not speak to the other, I spoke to myself. I apologized for creating the environment with the others, which caused them to behave that way with me. I asked for their forgiveness. I thanked them with my whole heart, and I sent love to them, and to myself. I did this every day for a few weeks. Incredibly, the relationships improved to such an extent that I was able to feel at peace and safe in their presence. These prayers can be used for everything in your life, not just problems. You can bring joy and happiness into your life, professional success, and abundance. You can fulfill your lifelong dreams. When you fully comprehend that YOU design your own life by your conscious and unconscious beliefs and desires, expectations, positive and negative thoughts, then you take back control. *Life is not happening to you, but because of you.* When we can be free from our past, we are permeated with Divine Intelligence and Love.

8 KUNDALINI AWAKENING

For over a year after the fear event, my body continued to vibrate at random moments, lasting anywhere from a few minutes to an hour. Most of the time, the vibrations were mild, but sometimes they were violent, causing my limbs to bounce and my teeth to chatter. My first instinct would be to brace for irrational anxiety. When that didn't come, I rode it out, waiting for limbs and system to calm. What was happening? Was it physical? Had I suddenly developed Parkinson's? I had always had a tremor, that usually affected my hands off and on. I had learned this was a release of energy for me. I had also been told by healers it could be caused by body trauma. I'd had a few head injuries as a small child. My intuition told me the vibrations were not physical, but spiritual. I hit the books again, to try and understand what was happening. When I entered my symptoms into the computer, the terms Kundalini Awakening[21] popped up.

---

21   Kundalini Awakening, according to www.anahana.com, is believed to be the ultimate goal and pinnacle achievement for

The phrase sounded familiar, but only that.

Kundalini is a Sanskrit word meaning "coiled snake." It refers to life-force energy resting at the base of our spine, often referred to as the divine feminine energy that resides within all things. When awakened, through yogic exercises, spontaneous awakening, or spiritually transformative experiences, the person can experience a myriad of symptoms including body shaking and uncontrollable jerking, feelings of intense cold or heat in various parts of the body, especially along the chakras, waves of wisdom and insight, strange internal sounds like buzzing or ringing. Kundalini energy moves up through the spine, through the chakras[22] and allows an individual to experience expanded forms of consciousness. Yogis believe an awakened kundalini brings states of lightness, joy, and bliss. It pulls the energy that lies dormant at the base of our spine up to the crown of our heads, creating an upward flow of energy and balancing our chakras and energetic bodies. I experienced most of them. The amount, type, and frequency of symptoms you receive depend on your own spiritual journey and any energetic

---

many seeking spiritual enlightenment. People who experience awakened kundalini, gain access to higher level consciousness and great awareness, leading to profound personal transformation and transcendence.

22   In Hinduism and Buddhism, chakras are focal points of energy/prana in the subtle/energy body. The exact number and location of chakras in the body, vary, depending on the tradition one follows.

blocks you may have. According to www.yogagroup.
org, there are approximately fifteen symptoms that can be
attributed to an awakening kundalini.

- o *A feeling of intense energy in the spine area* (can be
  felt as heat/vibration/electric – mine was intense
  vibrations/shaking/jerking movements)
- o *The sensation of heat or electric shocks moving from the
  spine to top of the head*
- o *Pain in the spine area and/or the tailbone* (coccyx) *area.*
  I experienced sharp pain in my sacrum and along my
  spine off and on. I cleared my chakras.
- o *The feeling of being overwhelmed.* (I experienced intense
  moments of anxiety and overwhelm which stopped
  me in my tracks)
- o *The need to release emotions* (I often released
  negative and repressed emotions through bouts of
  unexpected crying)
- o *Changes in diet and/or nutrition* (I became hyper
  focused on going non-gmo, researching ways to heal
  myself nutritionally, and lived a full year sugar free.)
- o *A feeling of being out of one's body* (I experienced
  a heightened state of awareness of being 8-10 feet
  tall, and felt I was walking in a different dimension
  for a few hours in 2016. I often experience this now
  in meditation).
- o *Having episodes of increased energy and productivity,*

experiencing euphoria (I don't recall the productivity, but I felt euphoric often).

o *Changes in sleep patterns* (I alternated between heavy sleep and waking often through the night)

o *Changes in sexual desire* (this occurred off and on during this time)

o *Changes in mood* (My mood fluctuated often through the day, creating difficulty for myself and my family)

o *A need for solitude* (I used to be outgoing, involved, said yes to everyone, volunteered for everything. This completely changed for me. I retreated into 'hermit mode.' My personality changed to a more introspective quiet. I pulled back from everything.

o *A need for creative expression* (I became interested in watercolor, poetry and began writing a spiritual blog).

o *An increased pull towards spiritual practice* (During and after my kundalini awakening, I completely let go of my Catholic beliefs, recognizing we are all One, the goal of our Soul is to attain Unity or Christ Consciousness while on Earth. I remembered I am on a Mystic path)

o *A feeling of being out of control* (This would hit me from time to time, feeling I had no control over the direction of my life, or what would happen next).

I was intrigued. When I began experiencing physical vibrations, it moved up my body from my upper thighs, through my trunk, my arms, to the base of my throat, but not to my crown. (This is meaningful and will be addressed in another chapter). Later, after I recovered and defeated the fear entity, the vibrations happened a few times a day, then once a day, then once every few days, and gradually happened less and less, until it stopped after a year. From this point forward, I began experiencing higher levels of conscious awareness which led to ongoing states of transcendence.

A few years ago, I woke suddenly in the middle of the night as my hands automatically positioned themselves into different movements. In consternation, I asked my Higher Self what was happening. The word "Mudras" came to me. I had never heard of that word. The next morning, I did an internet search and was astounded to discover not only was Mudra a real word, but it also held profound spiritual meaning. Mudras are an ancient set of energy-flowing postures using various placement of fingers, thumbs and palms to stimulate various parts of the body. I recognized the positions of Shuni (used to improve intuition, alertness and sensory powers, also purifies emotions and thoughts), the Dhyana (brings you into deeper, and more profound concentration, bringing tranquility and peace), and Vitarka, the Teaching Mudra, (allowing better reception to learning and personal growth).

When I experience moments of doubt of my path, of the messages I have received, I consider these events.

The mudras and kundalini happened spontaneously. I had no knowledge of them beforehand and after researching, discovered they are assisting my spiritual journey. I sit in amazement and wonder most of the time and can only continue, wondering what is next.

9 CONSTELLATION FAMILY THERAPY

A few months after battling the malevolent fear entity, I expressed readiness to my therapist, Joanne McAllister, to start the real work of healing. Her specialty was Family Constellation Therapy, a therapeutic approach developed by Bert Hellinger[23] to help reveal the hidden dynamics in a family relationship to address any stressors impacting these relationships and heal them. When something presents itself to be healed (like body trembling signaling to my conscious self), the healer we need appears.

Over the course of a few sessions, I learned the truth of my role within my family. Painful questions I'd had my whole life were answered and truth resonated for me.

---

23   Bert Hellinger was a German psychotherapist who, in the mid-1990's developed Family Constellation Therapy. He observed patterns of mental health concerns, illness, negative emotions, and potentially destructive behaviors within families. He suggested individuals might unconsciously adopt these concerns as a way of helping other members to cope.

Joanne mentioned the concept, I made my own realization. Emotional, behavioral, and psychological patterns continue in families with millennia of abuse. Even after emotional, physical, or sexual abuse stops, unconscious patterns of behavior, like 'victimhood,' continue into each succeeding generation. It takes incredible emotional and spiritual strength to overcome it. It takes a lightworker. I was born into my family specifically to stop generational cyclic patterns of abusive behavior and to permanently rid ourselves of the dark entity which had feasted on our fear and pain for hundreds if not thousands of years. Over the years, my three younger sisters and I fell into our own patterns with each other. Although I was the oldest, I was not treated that way. By remaining unobtrusive in the background, I played my own role. It wasn't until I began my own family, that I became painfully conscious of how often I felt unseen and unheard around my sisters and parents.

When I underwent Family Constellation therapy, our subconscious patterns of behavior with each other fell into place. There was no blame and my intuition of our interrelationship made sense. When I walked into the therapist's cozy office, she had me write the names of my immediate family members and myself on pieces of paper. After, she told me to place the names around the room, wherever felt right. Curious, I did this. Afterwards, she had me stand in whichever direction felt right, where I placed my name. She asked me to observe where I had placed the other members....my mom and dad....my sisters. Their placement spoke volumes to Joanne about how I saw myself in my family, in comparison with everyone else. While my sisters assumed their own unconscious roles from past generations, my role was to take on the burden of Victim. Incredible awareness and memory flooded me. At an early age, I felt I was no longer being taken care of. This is different from feeling unloved. I was well loved as a child and throughout my life. My mom was grappling with her own lifelong patterns of behavior. She passed the following unspoken understanding to me at an early age. *I had to take care of myself, and I had to take care of others before I took care of myself.* Most young people come to the first realization naturally in their older adolescence and young adulthood. It's a natural progression towards self-responsibility to live on our own. If this realization is forced too soon, when we still need a lot of care and attention, we can be traumatized. Over time, the trauma is buried, though we continue to act out learned behavior, harming ourselves and future relationships.

When I left home for college, I unknowingly sought 'to be taken care of.' I found it in my first boyfriend. For the first time in a long while, I received love and attention for just myself. I didn't have to earn it or share it with anyone. When he broke up with me, it wasn't a mere break up, he took away my security of care and attention. I was traumatized all over again and spent the next 3-4 years trying to re-establish 'care and attention' from my off and on boyfriend. I felt hurt by other's actions often. I unconsciously sought others' care and concern of me. I felt resentful of pets because they received constant care and attention. I know it was irrational and ridiculous. I was not aware of my feelings for a long time. Feeling overburdened remained until the Fear event, when I was forced to delve into my inner self.

I had taken on this Contract with family members before birth. During my STE, I took on the fear entity that had dogged my family through every generation. I have healed, and hope others in my family have as well. The work continues; it is not something that can be resolved overnight. Like an onion, when one layer of pain and trauma is healed, another layer is revealed. As recently as this past summer, I spontaneously let go of life-long emotional pain from family members, who were unconsciously playing out roles passed down from my mother's family, and her parents' families in continuum. As of this writing, most of the healing has occurred and is permanent.

10 HEALING THE BODY, MIND AND SPIRIT

My intuition was in overdrive after the 'event.' I began to know and understand each one of us can heal our own bodies of the illnesses and traumas we have received through our lives. There are many healing plants and medicines found in nature, as well as those developed by man. Alternative health therapies played a key role in helping support my system during the first three years after my spiritually transformative experience.

Allopathic (Western) medicine is important, and has established its place in healing, but should be balanced with Complementary medicine. Alternative medicine is intuitive medicine. Read that again. We know intuitively what our bodies need to heal. Unfortunately, we no longer trust our intuitive voice, and only trust outside more "authoritative" voices. Why is this? When did we stop trusting ourselves to know our own needs? I can answer this question in its most basic form; we have been taught for a millennium to fear our own selves! We have been taught not to trust ourselves, our thoughts, our feelings and "knowing." We have been conditioned to believe (by those in power) that others know more about our own selves than we do. Take your power back. Start paying attention. If your gut is telling you no...listen to it. Perhaps medical error and accidental overdosing could be prevented if we paid more attention. It's incredible to me that people do not trust to know what is best for themselves. Today, it takes a lot of courage to step out and say...'No! This is not what my body needs. I can heal myself. I can protect myself. I trust myself.' There is intense pressure from society, doctors, and Big Pharma to follow norms which don't necessarily apply to every single person and can harm us over time.

FUNCTIONAL MEDICINE

Healing the body is a multibillion-dollar industry. It is difficult to know who to listen to, or what health plan to follow. Through my own trials, I found functional medicine the best source of western medicine. Functional medicine treats the body as a whole system, rather than treating individual parts. Dr. Mark Hyman, best-selling author, speaker, and functional medicine practitioner provides thousands of hours of free information on YouTube, Podcasts, and other social media sites. If you are ready to heal your body, do some research. If a book or video resonates for you, listen to it. I love the phrase "take what you want and leave the rest."

I spent a lot of money on various diet plans, supplements, and private pay doctors to get the best advice on how to take care of my body, when truly, I only needed to ask myself what I needed. I experience a lot of inflammation throughout my body and discovered many of my 'go to' snack foods like cucumber and pineapple, fight inflammation. I have struggled with weight gain for half of my life. I've done the most ridiculous and extreme diets (like Phen Phen and the HCG Diet), along with almost every other fad diet. A few years ago, I decided to take back control, and completely changed how I eat. I went mostly GMO free, recognizing my body reacts strongly to glyphosate in foods. It was a lengthy process and took time. As recently as November 2023, I decided to jump start intermittent fasting and caloric restriction with a 4 day fast from all food. It wasn't as hard as I thought it would be, and it completely reset my body. I lost twelve pounds in 2 days (water weight) and have steadily let go of weight each week since then. Weight loss, when done according to our body's needs, is not difficult to accomplish. It requires trial and error, and patience.

When you listen to your body, you intuitively seek out what your body needs. Over the years, I have used cranio-sacral therapy, myofascial release, massage and Bowen therapy, shamanic healing, reiki, and other energetic healing methods with varying levels of success. When there are blockages within our bodies and we cannot heal ourselves with the knowledge we have, allopathic medicine is there to help support us. If you have a serious health concern, check with your doctor first, then research what you can do to help support your own healing.

COMMUNICATION WITH OUR BODY

Kryon, angelic beings channeled by Lee Carroll since 1989, have shared we have an Innate Body (or Smart Body) which holds its own intelligent consciousness. This 'smart body' is accessed through muscle testing, kinesiology, emotional freedom technique (EFT), acupuncture and pressure, and communicates directly with the body through our multidimensional DNA[24]. The innate body is responsible for spontaneous and miraculous healing. We can ask our body what it needs, and it will answer! I discovered that accessing my innate body by utilizing muscle testing[25] and EFT, was beneficial for identifying the most suitable foods for me and letting go of unhealthy connections with toxic individuals in my life. Imagine a scenario where medical school curricula included training for general practitioners

---

24   Kryon speaks of multidimensional DNA, which makes up 95% of DNA and needs to be activated. Chemical linear structures seen with scientific measurement make up only 5% of DNA. *The Twelve Layers of DNA; An Esoteric Study of the Mastery Within* by Kryon, 2010

25   Muscle testing can identify allergies and sensitivities, test for nutritional deficiency, assess emotional and psychological stress, assess energy imbalances, determine appropriate treatments needed, and is used in biofeedback and self-care.

in the use of kinesiology and muscle testing as an additional diagnostic tool, to assess our body's requirements for healing. We could prevent misdiagnosis, unnecessary surgeries and reduce the need for inappropriate medication.

Heal Your Body by Louise L. Hay is another excellent example of how we can use intuitive knowledge of our body to discover the cause of physical ailments and then work towards healing. Suppressed and ignored anger and rage can develop into painful debilitating stomach ailments. If not treated, they can become life threatening and cancerous. If you are experiencing pain, see a doctor, but also consider what you are feeling or experiencing in your life on a continued or chronic basis. Is there a friend, family member or lover who has angered you? Are you angry about your life and the unfulfillment of dreams? Do you feel there is no place for your anger? Is your stress and worry ongoing and overwhelming? Are you irrationally afraid? Talk to a therapist and get a journal. Ask yourself questions and listen for the answers. Your intuitive self may be rusty, but it is there waiting to communicate with you. The answer may come as images, songs, words, or other forms of inspiration. In meditation, you can ask to speak to your spiritual guide, and ask them questions about caring for yourself.

ANCESTRAL HEALING

My Family Constellation therapist had opened my eyes to family origin trauma and patterns repeating through succeeding generations. I sought the help of an incredibly gifted Medical Intuitive[26] named Amy. She was able to intuitively "see" everything within my energy field and clear anything presenting itself for healing. She educated me on ancient programs and contracts[27] I was still acting under and were impacting my life in negative ways. She uncovered a deeply held belief that I was unworthy of being loved or valued (quite common for empaths). This rooted program impacted me on every level growing up, causing me to hide or become silent when I was bullied or emotionally attacked. It also caused me to accept unacceptable behavior from people in my life, for fear I would lose their love and/or friendship. When I was young and squabbling with one of my sisters, she deeply wounded me with a thoughtless remark. I should have just brushed it off and moved on, understanding she was just trying to poke me. Instead, I was horribly crushed to my core. I believed her thoughtless words. Who was I to believe I deserved to be loved unconditionally? It took decades to heal from that.

A demoralizing program that wreaked havoc in my life revolved around the belief that, as a woman, I lacked

26   A Medical Intuitive can intuitively read the biofield of a person, scanning the physical, emotional, mental and spiritual body for energetic blockages and imbalances. The practitioner brings these imbalances to conscious awareness to help promote healing.
27   Subconscious programs and contracts are created from trauma to protect us from future hurt and pain and can be transferred unknowingly from one generation to the next.

a voice and that my wisdom went unnoticed by those in positions of authority. During Graduate school, when my thesis advisor yelled at me after reading the first two chapters of my thesis on UN reform, calling my fully researched work a "manifesto," I cowered. I believed my work was not worthy of notice. I gave up and walked away from my master's degree and two years' work within a nongovernmental organization working towards United Nations reform (to create a Citizen's Assembly within the United Nations, called the Global People's Assembly[28]). A survival mechanism created out of necessity and survival hundreds or thousands of years ago, was harming me now.

Piece by piece, the medical intuitive pulled out and healed each damaging thorn. Eventually I reached a point where I was cleared of the unconscious programs and contracts, but it took a willingness to suspend disbelief in something I didn't understand. It took faith, and patience. As I cleared ancient programs, my self-esteem and self-worth grew tremendously. People, including some family members and friends, who had always treated me from the place of my program (like being unworthy of attention, or believing my work was not worth considering), were bemused by changes occurring within me. In many instances, I had

---

28   Global People's Assembly founded by Dr. Lucille Green who was a Global Visionary dedicated to democratizing and empowering the United Nations for the purpose of creating a more just, sustainable, and hopeful future for humanity.

to cut energetic cords to be released from their unhealthy attachments and behavior with me.

Newly discovered Epigenetics[29] proposes that emotional and physical trauma can be held in cells of the body and passed down through generations. Epigenetics is real, based upon my own experiences, those of family members and our known ancestral history. As more research is done, evidence will change everything in how we recognize and heal inherited emotional, psychological, and physical injuries to the body and mind. The health ramifications are boundless! This is preventative medicine.

ENERGY CORD CUTTING

Everything is made of energy. In physics, energy is the capacity for doing work. When energy transfers from one body to another, it heats up. Often, when a healer collaborates with a patient, the patient can feel heat radiating from their hands. In spirituality, energy refers to an interpersonal, non-physical force or essence. Books and articles have been written about the varying forms of spiritual energy. One book which had a profound effect on my perception is James Redfield's A *Celestine Prophecy*.

You may have read his books, or even seen the movie of the same name. It is an excellent layperson's explanation of what spiritual energy is, and how it works within not just the

---

29   More information in Resources at back of this book.

body, but through every living thing. Everything has energy. Some things vibrate at such a low rate, it is indiscernible (a rock), others at such a high rate it cannot be seen with the naked eye (light). In *The Celestine Prophecy*, the main character discovers how to see auras[30] (spiritual energy) around people, plants, trees, and animals. He sees how the energy moves back and forth between two people when they interrelate, how it can change color depending on the moods of the individuals and the quality of conversation. Angry or frustrated energy are dark reds, spiky, and frenetic. Calm, loving, and peaceful colors are soft blues, greens, pinks, and yellows.

I was especially interested in how feeling energy moves between individuals, like the empathic experiences I had had throughout my life. When we start to communicate with another, an energetic cord (imagine a silvery cord) connects us. Information runs along this cord, sharing non-verbal information about each other. If you are good at visualization, you can sense where the cord is placed on your body, you can "see" what it looks like, or you can "sense" what it feels like. The 'rope' can be of different thickness and textures. For myself, when I look within for the connector, it can be different textures like a steel cable or a piece of string or a strong fishing line. It depends on how strong your connection is to the other. This person could have a

---

30   An Aura is a colored energy field that emanates around a body. Many healers can see the state of being and health of a client, based on the vibration, size and color of the aura.

strong attachment to you, and just be an acquaintance. If that person is draining you of your energy (you feel it as weakness, tiredness, discomfort, stress when you are around that person), they could have 'placed' a strong cord. If you continue to be unaware of it, it can impact your life in negative ways. I will give you a personal example.

When they were young, my children swam on a recreational team in our town. While the kids swam their hearts out, parents milled around chatting with each other or encouraging their kids on the sidelines. Sometimes we could be there for hours if we had multiple children swimming. For the most part, I had a good relationship with everyone. Sometimes I met people who were confused or instinctually resisted my spiritual understanding of their true self. Unconscious fear and confusion lead to anger. Not understanding the spiritual cause, they react by bullying. There was a woman who did not like my son for some reason. She made nasty comments about his ability and whether he should be on the team or alluded to him being a bully of her son. She was popular with the other parents, and slowly they stopped talking to me. It really upset me, though I tried hard to distance myself from her. After a few weeks of this, I decided to cut energy cords with her. I closed my eyes and asked to see the cord between us. It was not a large cord, but it did have a little bit of steel to it. Her condemnation of me triggered my program of 'not being worthy of love.' It had sunk in its hooks.

I spoke to the cord, telling it I forgave her for the hurtful angry things she had said. I sent compassion and love to her, and while I did that, visualized bolt cutters, and cut the cord. It took some time as it didn't snap immediately. Eventually it sprang away, back to the lady. I healed the spot it had been attached to with healing green light. The next swim practice, and every practice after that, the energy around her completely shifted. I could sense her confusion, as she tried to get my attention, but I was no longer invested in it. I felt lighter and happier. It was amazing. I never had an issue with her again, and much later, she reached out to me with kindness. Cord cutting is highly effective. It is important not to allow cords to attach to us after any communication between you and another is over. Even cords attached to beloved family members should be released after communicating. It does not lessen the love we share. The more you practice it, the more in tune with your energetic body you will be.

I have used energy cord cutting often over the years, and each time I am surprised by how quickly the emotional or spiritual issue is resolved afterwards. Most recently, I healed myself of a very painful spot on my upper left chest, near my collarbone. It was agonizing and I began to believe I would have it the rest of my life. I prayed and meditated about this pain, and the answer came to me one day. There was obviously a deeper emotional and spiritual component to this pain than mere physical. In *"Heal Your Body"* Louse Hay described my shoulder pain as 'carrying the burden of life, feeling helpless and hopeless.' She also described joint pain as 'representing changes in direction in life and the ease of these movements.' This blew me away. I'd been making major changes in my life; I had started writing this book and was a little fearful of where my life was headed. I was also feeling helpless and hopeless about my extended family dynamic. It has been a source of incredible emotional pain. I have changed so much from the person I had been before awakening, that my family does not know how to relate to me. I sense their confusion, anger, and sadness. They don't understand why I have changed, and believe I am careless of causing strife within the family. How could I explain myself? I felt hopeless about it.

When I became aware of the need to cut energetic cords, I asked my guides whom I needed to cut them. Immediately, one of my family members came to me. We struggled often through our lives. Her cord was attached to the most painful spot, the upper front left side of my shoulder. The spiritual cause has to do with my heart, specifically the grief I felt at the emotional loss of her. It was heartbreaking and kept me in pain. As soon as I recognized, and the cord presented to me, I was able to let it go. It took time, as it was formed, not of soft or metal material, but of sinew. It had grown into me and when unattached, felt like I was disconnecting muscles. I peeled away piece by piece, all the while sending love, compassion, and forgiveness to her. Immediately the pain stopped. Just like that. The pain has not returned. I was flummoxed. This was miraculous! I could heal myself! This was not a theory or wishful thinking. Even more amazing, I experienced Grace. All the pain, hurt, confusion, anger, disbelief, disempowerment, hopeless feeling that surrounded our relationship, completely dissolved. All I felt was love. Unconditional compassionate love. I let her go, and it was ok. That has remained as well.

Soul to the World

11   REIKI

For a few years after my traumatic fear event, I thought a lot about other ways to heal myself. In my teens, I'd been inspired and deeply affected by a story[31] of a woman who had been killed in a car accident and came back to life with healing abilities. She healed herself of paralysis and was able to heal others by taking on their pain temporarily. Although it was not a true story, I felt it could have been. I intuitively sensed every person can heal themselves and support other's healing. We had only forgotten how.

By this point, I continued having pain in my lower back (from a sledding accident in my twenty's), my neck (caused by birth trauma), and various aches and pains through my body[32]. I was frustrated I didn't know the spiritual cause or how to reverse it. I'd had my gallbladder removed and

---

31   The 1980 movie *Resurrection* with Ellen Burstyn tells the story of a woman who, after dying in a car crash, came back to life with miraculous healing abilities.

32   I'd been born with a shortened sternocleidomastoid muscle which had been surgically removed at age 16. It created varying forms of pain throughout my neck, shoulders and back over my life.

still experienced pain from scarring and inflammation. In the Spring of 2013, I flipped through a wellbeing magazine and found a Reiki[33] master named Beverly Farris who had been trained by Takata. Takata was trained by Usui, the first Master of Reiki. For those knowledgeable of reiki, this was extremely valuable. Knowledge and training are passed down from Master to student. Each student remembers the chronology of master's before them. While talking with her, I shared my awakening journey. She shared about an awakening workshop that delved deeper into the spiritual process than reiki provided. There was a great deal of unresolved trauma from the fear event that needed healing, beyond my own abilities. I intuitively knew this Master and her training and workshop would complete my healing from the event three years ago.

Before studying to become a first and second level reiki practitioner, I attended their "Awakening to your Self" workshop. Carla Allison, one of the facilitators, worked with Beverly to help guide us through two parts. In the first, they discussed support, healing, and spiritual understanding we could attain. While sitting and listening, my lower body began trembling, sometimes noticeably, sometimes inwardly.

---

33   Reiki is a rediscovered ancient healing technique by Dr. Usui Nikao. A practitioner lays hands on a patient, using life force energy that flows through the practitioner into the patient, helping to clear energy blockages and resume natural energy flow.   It treats the whole body, mind, emotions, and spirit. Many have reported miraculous healing results.

I could not control it. I raised my hand and told them (and the room of approximately a dozen people) of my awakening process and the event. I explained my trembling and let them know I was eager to find answers to my questions. Carla and Beverly exchanged knowing glances and with a smile, Carla began "you are already awakened. You are seeking to create a connection with your Higher Self, consciously, and uncover your gifts, but you've been stopped." This floored me. Confirmation again of my intuition. We had been doing grounding exercises, then pulling energy up our bodies and through our crowns. I began experiencing aching, shooting pain around the back of my neck. (a decade before, I'd had a Shaman remove dark brown looking pellets from my neck through spiritual means. He stated they had been placed there in a previous life. I'd had pain at the back of my neck for years). After learning about my experience, Carla and Beverly stated "we don't normally do this in an information session, but you are presenting to us energies that are ready and need to be cleared. Do you give us permission?" I nodded with interest. It is essential to receive permission before treatment, to respect the free will of an individual.

They had me sit in the center of a seated circle with reiki healers facing me. Beverly stood behind me and Carla worked in front. As they worked the energy in my energy field, Carla asked me questions about different areas of my body...injuries I had experienced at young ages I had forgotten about. I was amazed by their spot-on intuition. I asked about the ongoing discomfort I received from the left side of my body. They stated the left side of the body represented our Female aspect. I had experienced many difficult past lives as a woman. I asked about the trembling. They said it was how my physical body chose to bring my need for healing, to my conscious awareness. It was also a gage for energy awareness.

Carla told me what was happening in different areas of my energy field[34]. Her statements confirmed information I've known or suspected. She asked how I was feeling in my throat, and I stated "thick." She said there were a lot of blockages there. I had spent many lifetimes suppressing my truth, not expressing myself, holding myself back...sometimes for fear of my life. She cleared most of it out and got the rest later during the main workshop. (Of interest, my umbilical cord was wrapped around my neck before I was delivered. Intuition led my delivery doctor to reach in and pull the cord off before it strangled me at birth. I can't wear necklaces, or I get a rash (metal allergy).) She told me to expect to feel free

---

34   The energy field has been studied by medical scientists since 1938 with Harold Burr and his study of "Life Fields". He described the energy or "Life" field as an electro-dynamic field (around the body) which can be seen to vary in health and disease. From a spiritual perspective, the energy field that surrounds a human is called the Merkabah (Light-Spirit-Body) and holds everything of relevance to our soul.

to express myself from this point and to pay attention when my habitual action would be to "take it back." In the past, I would always look for confirmation from others that my thoughts or beliefs were "ok." Since the workshop, when I state something, I leave it, and let others make up their own mind about it. I've been tempted often to pull back my words, not say them, or soften my words to make others feel better. It's been a challenge to own my truth. When I do, it's very self-empowering. I am still working on it. Later that evening, when my trembling presented for more work, they addressed the heart of the matter.

Since beginning my awakening process in the early 1990's, I have always sensed a heaviness/empty void that has blocked me from full life experience. I once had a gifted healer and physical therapist describe this heaviness to me while working on my upper back and neck. She sensed a heavy weight, like a dark depression, which hung around the back of my neck, but was separate from me. I was not depressed, but this energy was "depressing" my energy and life force. I had always sensed this through my high school and college years, although I never allowed myself to fall into it. I knew it was "other," I just didn't know where it came from or how to rid myself of it. It would often feel like an attack on my spirit. I spoke to many healers, psychics, and self-help teachers like Esther Hicks/Abraham[35] and Dr.

---

35   Abraham is a spiritual being or group of beings channeled by Esther Hicks to help humanity uncover their own Truth and realize we

Wayne Dyer[36] to try and remove the "block" (as I came to call it). I continually received the messages "the knowledge was within" and "I could heal myself when I was ready." It was so frustrating because I had no idea how to heal myself then. My usual methods of journaling, talk therapy and physical therapy were not effective.

During one of the workshop sessions, my neck and left shoulder began to hurt a lot. I could not raise my Chi/energy past my throat. It was blocked. The facilitators and a few other reiki healers stated I had what looked like glass shards stuck in my neck. I was able to intuitively see them as well. It was a remnant of the dark entity I battled from my fear event. I stated, "they are holding me in place." This was very meaningful. During the clearing/healing of this block, I clairvoyantly saw that this dark entity had been in my family for generations. It went all the way back to the start of my family line...pre-history. That fear event I'd had was the human experiences of this entity through my entire family line. It had been creating horrific situations with family members, to feed on our fear and rage. {Through work with my therapist, I discovered the faint and broken words I had spoken during that first night came from the memories of a young ancestor who was brutalized and buried alive}.

all have the power to heal ourselves and live our best lives.
36   Dr. Wayne Dyer was an internationally renowned author and speaker in the fields of self-development and spiritual growth. He wrote more than 40 books over four decades, including 21 New York Times bestsellers.

I drained the entity and let go of it permanently. As it left my body, I felt an overwhelming physical sensation of pain, aching, dragging, weakness, moving down from my neck, through my body, down my legs, and into the earth, to dissipate into nothingness. The block was gone. I knew what I experienced was real. It was all a confirmation of the work I'd done with therapist friend, Joanne, and my Constellation work. The neck pain has never returned.

After the Awakening workshop, I went home and fell into a deep meditation. So much information flooded through, and I sought to calm my mind and heart. When I came out of the meditation, I experienced an urgent need to sit down with paper and pen. My mind was blank, but my pen flew. The following message is a clarion call to my heart and soul. Let it speak to you.

I am the Way Shower
I am the Lightbringer
I am Teacher
I am here to help show the Way

I am here to bring a message of hope, of peace, of love, of release of anger, which doesn't serve any longer.

I am the Tree of Life. I am the Tree. I am the Roots. I am the Trunk. I am the Branches. I am the Leaves. I am the Veins of lifegiving energy and force. My Tree bears the Fruit of Love. My Branches grow, to encompass the whole world, weaving intricate and yet simple designs, mapping out new terrain, reemerging with the whole.

I am the Vein of Life which pulses through everything. I pulse through the very fabric of the universe of every universe. I am the Whole and I am the One Part.

The power of the Way flows within me. The Way is shown to me. The Pulse of Life is our heartbeat thrumming with energy, waves of peace (that flow) from each being, whether aware or not. Pulsing, I am the light and the darkness.

I grow with Her. I am Mother Gaia. I am the Truth, the Way. I am the Gather. I am the Disciple. I am governed by all of you. I am the whisper of wind as a beetle, flies over a stalk of grass. I am the crash of ocean waves. I arrive in peace. I begin to show my Way and with me, all of you, to begin the process of knowing. You are all here on this journey, a preparation, a celebration, a peaceful re-affirming, or a din, a crash of sound, to be heard over the beating of your fearful hearts.

I will pound the truth out of you if I need to. I will awaken the Truth within you in the many ways at My disposal. You are Mine to move mountains with. You are the Way Shower. You will lead them back to Me. Bring them to realization. Bring the Light of knowing back into their eyes, so that they may see Me again.

I know we are all one. Many parts of the Whole. It is simple. Be the Way.

12   PROGRAMS

When it comes to healing, there is no "one stop shop." You need more than one kind of therapist. You need various kinds of healers, depending on the inner work you've been presented with. As one layer is healed and let go, another layer is revealed. You can't force the process; the healer will show up when needed. As I delved deeper into my emotional trauma and pain, I began to work with "Amy" (the medical intuitive) more often. I had been struggling with blocks and obstacles to my healing. The intuitive shared we all work under ancient contracts and programs put into place for survival from our past lives, but which still play out in our present. The following programs and effects on my life, are paraphrased from Amy's words.

WOMAN AND RELATIONSHIP PROGRAM

What I have been feeling lately, is the Collective Pain of Women, for thousands and thousands of years. It carries a personal element for me. The issues of forgiving myself and others, fear, and avoidance of seeing truth, fear of moving forward, are collective female energy. I'm frozen in place and can't create. I'm paralyzed. I'm too heavy, there is too much. My body can't carry the weight. I'm feeling old stuff, from my whole life and past lives. These constrictions have always been there, but now that I am receiving spiritual support, I'm starting to feel them in my body. It's my left side (female) that I experience most of my physical issues. Everything is so heavy and painful. I've been carrying these life stories within my body; the Belief and Program of a woman being a Slave, Sold, Owned. I don't know who owns me, so I haven't been able to let it all go. I have been Bound. This occurred in a past life and has been reoccurring ever since. The specific energy from this experience comes from the "history level.' I've been trying to resolve this heavy stuff my whole life. Now I have help, the heaviness and pain are coming up fast and intense.

My Female Program is cultural, legally enforced and a "mindset of the times." This feeling like I can't escape. My system doesn't recognize any way out of it. My soul has been yearning/seeking a way out. To be Free. My entire system is in Lockdown.

There is a Blood Oath I made in the past. It was an actual blood oath (not metaphor), committing my life to my husband/partner. I was excited about it...it was expected of me and all women. I was not coerced. He was a good man and powerful. The belief in being a man's property was conditioned for thousands of years. My energy feels "owned" by this Binding Blood Oath. It was a ritual blood oath with a god. It goes back into our ancient pagan past. It was considered a normal marriage ritual. In marriage, I became owned. Wife equaled Slave/Property.

We both 'entered' this promise together. He (my husband now is the same soul I bound myself to then) is just responding to 'things' as they have always been. It is not his fault. He did not set out to own me, per se, it was just the way it was done then. It is time to be resolved, for both of us.

We've been "at war" with each other. It's been so unnecessary, and I am stepping out of the 'war.' We need to be with each other coming from compassion and gratitude. There is a reason we keep finding each other and feel compelled to be together. Our relationship has been co-dependent, because we couldn't manage to resolve this, although we wanted to. We are good together when this is not an issue. We are equal partners. My truth of who my real self is, is compatible with his true self.

Up until now, I couldn't move forward without his permission, and he hasn't given it! I have permission to move forward. I have a right to own myself!

The program of "The Fall" goes back to Adam and Eve. Old programming is the basic fabric upon which our human mythology of relationships between men and women is built. There cannot be trust, equality or real love when this program is in place. The feeling of "entitlement," "ownership," or a "hierarchy," gets in the way of the higher Law of Love. "They" killed Jesus (Yeshua) specifically because He taught people to Love. He told them to stop following rules and just love each other. It was immensely powerful. The government shut it down because the people couldn't be controlled.

Love is becoming safer to experience now. There is freedom to learn equality and how to love. Women are free (in most countries). Women are powerful. We own ourselves only. No one can take my power. I am free. I own myself. Love is mutual respect and equality. The beginning of moving in a loving direction means I get to choose who I am. I am not in control, and I let it all go.

RAISING CHILDREN PROGRAM

We have a fear of the Wild. There is a subconscious need for things/people to be broken. We can't appreciate our children's "wildness." We see it as a problem that must be disciplined into proper behavior (instinctual survival mechanism). We need to appreciate their wildness. We need to treat them only with kindness and compassion, instead of being rule enforcers all the time. By only following rules, they become angry and mean. By experiencing our love, joy, compassion, and kindness, they want to emulate it for themselves. They learn to control themselves (and should be given freedom to make mistakes, so they may learn).

We've been focusing on the wrong stuff by trying to "break" them. Having a lot of energy is not bad. It does not need to be corrected or medicated. We need to give them space and freedom to expend their energy. We need to respect others and where they are. Be kind. We are afraid for our kids when they behave wildly. (An ancient program of needing to protect our children from danger). We want to break their spirits and make them 'obey.' When those kids grow up, they/we spend the rest of their lives trying to regain that part of themselves that was crushed in childhood. It is the cause for depression, illness, stress, disease, and mental illness in our teens and adulthood. We need to put our energy only towards the positive. Feel gratitude in every moment. Let go of the need to analyze and control the kids. We can let go of other people's old program expectations. You can't argue with Love.

***

When I began having my own children, I experienced this push/pull of their spirit and my own. I am sad to say in my boys' early years, when they were their most "wild," I tried to curb their wildness. I tried to get them to be acceptable to others' expectations, and to my own. I was raised with a lot of love and freedom, but there were unspoken expectations also. Fortunately, I was easy to raise, so didn't experience the crushing expectation that many kids today feel. Eventually, I recognized the incredible gift my boys' wildness was, and gave them freedom. I received a lot of censure from well-meaning friends and family, but I am happy to say, my children are well rounded. They are secure in my love and have courage to be themselves in a world that would punish them for that. I also have an excellent relationship with them.

There is a difference between providing a safe space for a child to be themselves, and just allowing a child to do whatever they want with no ramifications. There are natural consequences. When a child experiences those...let them feel it, do not try to protect them from it (although we can be supportive and compassionate while they go through it). If we step in to intervene too early, we don't do them or ourselves any favors in the long run.

Imagine what kids today would be like, if we let go of all the expectations we grew up with, of how they "should" behave, and just let them be themselves? I know people are inherently good. Children are the closest to our True Home...and are examples to us, to remember who we truly are. Why do we try to crush that? What does that say about our society? Just something to think about. I believe this could be the end of high school shootings, teen suicides, depression, gang fighting and murder. So many benefits could be had, if only we had the courage to completely change how we raise our children, and ourselves.

PART III
SOUL REMEMBRANCE

You are being prepared for an immense journey into Spirit.

-My Higher Self, 2016

Soul to the World

13   WAYSHOWER

In my early years of spiritual study, I desperately sought an answer to why I was so different from most. I had never met anyone like me. It was very isolating and left me feeling a bit crazy at times. Why was I so aware of other's emotions more than my own? Why did I feel a deep certainty I was here on Earth for an important purpose or mission? Why was it so easy to forgive and love those who had hurt me so much? Where did my certainty that everyone on Earth was intrinsically the same inside, and that truly we were all One together, come from? Why was I here and what was I supposed to be doing?! I knew that my "big mission" would be happening later in my life, but what was I supposed to do until then?

One day I wandered into a metaphysical bookstore near my college. I made a wide berth around the occult section. That had never interested me beyond curiosity. I perused interesting book titles like *You Can Heal Your Life!* by Louise L. Hay, *Celestine Prophecy* by James Redfield, and

Manifest Your Destiny by Dr. Wayne Dyer. These names meant nothing to me at the time. I eventually recognized that spiritual teachers and books come to you when you need them. Sometimes books can sit on your bookshelf for years before you are ready for their wisdom. In two years from that moment, I would discover and later meet Dr. Wayne Dyer. His beautiful and inspirational words and outlook on life would begin to transform mine. He was one of my 'guideposts.'

I meandered over to the counter and rifled through some angel cards the shop owner put out for customers to review. I pulled out a card randomly and read it. Goosebumps went up and down my arms. I felt a rush of energy unlike anything I'd ever experienced and took a step back.

You Are a Lightworker

I immediately asked the shopkeeper if she had any books about Lightwork and she directed me to Dr. Doreen Virtue's "*The Lightworker's Way.*" It had just been released in 1997, the same year I discovered it. Dr. Virtue's description of a Lightworker lit me up! According to Dr. Virtue,

"You are a Lightworker if you...

o   Feel called to heal others
o   Want to resolve the worlds social and environmental problems
o   Believe that spiritual methods can heal any situation
o   Have had mystical experiences, such as psychic pre-

monitions or angelic encounters

o   Have endured harsh life experiences that eroded the knowledge of your divine perfection

o   Want to heal your own life as a first step in healing the world

o   Feel compelled to write, teach or counsel about your healing experiences

o   Know you are here for a higher purpose, even if you are unsure what it is or how to fulfill it."

If you search online for the word "Lightworker," there are hundreds if not thousands of articles, websites, and YouTube videos describing what a Lightworker is, "signs" you are one, and so forth. I find Dr. Virtue's list to the point and answered my question...who am I? I identified with every single item on that list. Along with many psychic experiences, I'd had an angelic/divine encounter while in college. More recently, I found spiritual professionals writing about various kinds of Lightwork[37] such as Way Shower. A Way Shower is a high vibrational being of light who answers the Call to come to Earth and incarnate as a human. After remembering their true selves, their mission is to inspire, hold space and bring witness to humanity's awakening to their own True Selves. When we are able permanently, to live at a higher vibration, we show the

---

37   According to Souls Space (10/9/2019) there are 10 different types: Divine Lightkeepers, Gatekeepers/Grid Workers, Healers, Transmuters, Messengers, Seers/Psychics/Clairvoyants, Dreamers or Astral Travelers, Ascension Guides, Wayshowers, Divine Blueprint Creators and Manifesters (www.souls-space.com)

Way of Unity/Christ Consciousness. I am on this journey.

My Guides and Higher Self have been preparing me for my next step in the evolution of my Soul. Like a finely tuned instrument, I was being tuned to receive and experience higher levels of awareness and being. In November of 2013, I asked again, for what was I being prepared? Their answer came to me quickly.

Your mission on Earth is to help awaken, and to write. Your mission is to help people transition. When you combine them together, you will touch others and they in turn can touch the lives of others, and so on. You can be a flame to their match.

You seek the answers of God and Man. You seek to know that which you know already. You seek to understand the wisdom of the ancients, in a way that is easy for you to comprehend. You seek to believe that which is unbelievable, with your heart, and not with your mind. You seek joy and friendship with those who would be seen by you. You seek to be the True Messenger that you are. You seek to find a way to become this messenger in your daily life as well as on a larger scale. You are seeking so hard; you haven't been taking time to realize the answers are already within you and have been for some time. You need to believe in yourself, to believe in others. You will find the time to do this now. You are Messenger. You are Way Shower. Show them the Way.

You are ready to begin your next grand adventure. We believe you are ready. You must allow it to enfold you. You must open your heart chakra and allow what is within you to become you. Allow yourself to be taken over by it. Do not allow your fear to hold sway over your heart anymore. You have all the knowledge you need to begin this next phase of your life. Try and release anxiety. Breathe through anything you may be feeling. The time is now. You feel a building power within you to start.

You sense momentous change on this planet. All the pieces are being moved into position. You are sensing a tremendous buildup of energy. The exact moment is not known. Only God/Source knows exactly when Source/God will be sending out the wave[38] of power and energy that will transform humanity into the next level of consciousness. When the time comes, you will know exactly what you are here for. You will sense and know with absolute certainty what you are to do.

You are a Way Shower, as was given to you by Metatron[39]. You are here to be witness to the light in others, so they may find their way to the portal of Light.

You have taken a difficult path; one few souls were able to take. It is a strenuous road, but you are doing very well. Soon, your hard work will have paid off. For, we are always with you. You

---

38   reference to the 'energy wave' many channelers are perceiving, that will begin the Great Change of humanity's tremendous evolutionary leap in consciousness.

39   Metatron, an archangel (Light Being), known for guarding the Tree of Life, thought to exist as human (Enoch) before he ascended to become "King of Angels". Said to guard the Book of Life (Akashic Records), found within Kabbalah text

chose not to know and experience, so that you could speed up your own process. Going blind as it were. Soon, your shield will be taken from you, and you will See as you have sought to see and be seen. There is much important work for you to do still, and in that, the Way will be made clear to you. Trust you are exactly where you are meant to be. Your Father and Mother are (in great interest) with you. Jenny, you are an Ascended Master. Yes, believe it to be true, for you are one. You have not allowed yourself to know this consciously, because of the work you needed to do. Your sense of importance, which you are constantly trying to shield yourself from, is your own resistance to what you know to be true. Trust your own wisdom and inner guidance. When the time is right, you will know truly Who you are.

After receiving incredible divine knowledge of my True Self over the past five years, my heart has been stirred, and awareness floods. Everything happened in my life for a Purpose. Just as I'd intuited as a small child, everything I have gone through has been preparing me for my present and my future. Every mistake I made and learned from. My decades of physical pain and successful healing. Recognizing emotional pain from my family and I and healing it. Triumphantly overcoming all supernatural challenges from the fear event. Experiencing Grace through healing of personal relationships. I was being prepared in ways I had no idea of, then. Only in retrospect, can we see the obvious truth.

14   GUIDANCE

It is common, during our awakening and ascension process, to reach a point where nothing seems to be happening. We undergo a "Dark Night of the Soul." We've done tremendous inner healing work, experienced physical symptoms like kundalini vibrations and mysterious physical ailments that end when we become consciously aware of the root. We have aligned with our Higher Selves. We are firmly on our Path, and then.... nothing. We forget to trust the process. There comes a point where we fall back into old patterns of anger, fear, depression, and apathy. Doubt creeps in. We pull into ourselves, questioning this path we find ourselves on, wondering if it's real or just our imagination. Our friends and family (who didn't leave us initially) do not understand who we are becoming, and question whether we need to go to the hospital, find a good therapist, or get into a new line of work. I'd like to tell you this only happens once, but it is cyclical. We reach a certain level of understanding, and then we go through the arduous work all over again. If we haven't completely lost hope, we do eventually recognize we are in a completely different space than before. It takes less and less time to recognize where we are and heal the hurt. I started to see these as "tests" of the Spirit. Was I ready to move forward?

I started to question my spiritual path around the Spring of 2014. I spent time online, reading posts from other spiritual groups, those who suggested they were on the way to "ascension[40]" to the Fifth[41] Dimension. (Sounds like a great movie title). Those "special few" on spiritual websites and blogs discussed how and when people would begin ascending to the fifth dimension Easter week of 2014! The time was at hand! I read these words or words like these in multiple "credible" sites. Everyone believed it was the start of the "Event." There was a global sense the Event was like the Christian Rapture, where all the 'enlightened little souls of the world' would be 'taken' and sent to a better place (a shiny new Earth) all at once. Some well-known channelers informed their audience they were leaving and wouldn't return. All the channeled messages online were giving timelines. I knew that was wrong. Their vehement insistence "the time is Now! We are all ascending Now!"

40   Ascension is a natural soul process and state of being where we 'move' from one energetic vibrational level to the next. (i.e., 3rd to 5th dimension, understanding 4th dimension is Time). Matias DeStefano explains this best (see Resources at back of book).

41   5th Dimension, as described by spiritual channelers, is a state of pure Love and Being, where we fully embody our True Selves and live within Christ Consciousness on Earth.

made no sense. I became disheartened thinking either I was not "chosen" or not "ready" for ascension, or…it was all BS in the first place which was depressing to think about. I was in a dark place for a while; angry, irritable, disgusted and sometimes apathetic. Was it just not for me? Was I not worthy? My old program again! Our self-worth is unchangeable and unconditional. It is innate.

But, still, I felt an urge within me not to let go of my knowledge and intuition, of what I knew to be real. I let go of all that was going on around me and tried to stay centered within my own self. One night, as I was settling into sleep, I asked my guides 'can I see what is happening? Will you show me? Can I start experiencing what I know is real?' Early the next morning, I woke up around 4:30 am, went to the bathroom and went back to bed. I don't recall falling back to sleep, but suddenly I was in a different place.

I discovered myself sitting on my living room couch. I looked up and a very tall and familiar looking woman with several companions, stood above me. She reached her hand down to me. They were seven or eight feet tall. I felt very small (and I am a tall woman). The woman looked older, with short wavy white hair, and tanned skin. She and her companions radiated very loving, joyful, and peaceful energy. I sensed she was incredibly wise. I went with her, and we walked into a large kitchen. It was large and airy, with green plants hanging in a window and a massive wooden table and chairs. It felt very welcoming and cozy. My chin reached the top of the table! She asked if I'd like tea and went to make some. As she was puttering, she told me she had something for me to look at. I looked down, and there was a large spiral bound paper scrapbook. It had letters on it that, at the time, I recognized as belonging to me. I had the sense this was a book of my life. I opened the first page and was transported to a new place.

I stood in a large room/space which felt like a grand ballroom but with open walls to a large flowering yard. There were people I 'knew' all around me. A tall blond man in a white outfit stood to my right. I couldn't make out his features but had a keen sense he was my Guide. I felt emanations of love, protection, acceptance, and peace from him. I looked and vividly saw two of my sisters in front of me. As soon as they saw me, they came, hugging me, excited and happy I was there. My sisters were full of vital energy...glowing even. My children were all around me, laughing, dancing, and bouncing about. My oldest son was happy but quiet, my middle son was running, and my youngest daughter was bouncing and laughing. I was led towards what felt like a covered patio in the outside space.

My Guide brought a beautiful black dog up to me. Its coat and head were sleek, silky, and beautiful. He reminded me of a greyhound but full of soft and thick hair. My dog was very loving. In the next moment, I was in a new room/space.

It felt like a large 'old world' living room you might find in a large log cabin or the Old West. There were tall ceilings with wood beams, burnished dark wood furniture, off white painted walls, cozy throw rugs and pillows. In the distance, I could see another room/hall that had a large, polished wood staircase leading upstairs. I looked around the room and saw my mother. She was so vibrant. Her eyes were glowing with love, joy, excitement, wisdom, recognition of where were were...so much. I had been feeling very emotional through this whole experience, and when I saw her, I burst into joyful tears. We hugged each other deeply. I was saying, "It's been you!" I recognized we had been with each other for a long time. I eventually looked up and saw a man climbing the stairs. It was my dad, but his face kept going from young, to old, to young. I asked why his face didn't remain young, and she told me he was still in the process of Transformation.

It struck me then, where I was. I suddenly knew I was in a higher dimension. All these people had transformed/awakened to who they truly are and were here in this place with me. We, humanity, are all transforming, and coming to this new place, this higher dimension. Ultimately, we are all moving at our own pace, as we are ready to do so. I knew this was a real place. I also knew I was not in Heaven, in the sense that is where you go when you leave your body. I was here in my present body, vibrating at a much higher level. I remember looking around, feeling the table, looking at the

things that were grounded to Earth and saying to myself...
"it is real. This is a real place. I'm not dreaming. This is not
a dream."

The tall woman said, "you must have many
questions." I answered yes! I had so many. Before I could
really formulate one, she answered it by saying, *"Jenny, you
are on your Path. You've been on it all along. It's difficult for you
to realize, because there are those around you who do not recognize
they are on a path, and do not acknowledge you yourself are on
one. Because of this, you often feel lost. You are not lost. This
knowledge is now within you."*

My husband stirred beside me, and I felt myself being
'pulled back' to my sleeping body. Startled, I said to the woman
"Oh no, I'm being pulled back! I don't want to leave yet, I have
so many more questions, there is so much more to see." I had
a powerful sense of what was just beyond my vision. I tried to
stay. She and everyone told me I would be back. In a strange
trance, my physical body got up, used the restroom, and then
returned to my bed. I felt like I was walking in two worlds, here
and not here. I was with her and my Guide. I turned to him
and asked his name. *"My name is Daniel,"* he said with love. It
was given telepathically. I felt joy in knowing his name. I'm
grateful he showed himself to me. The lady reaffirmed I would
return, reassuring me that I was indeed in a real place. Then I
woke up fully, beside my husband.

Whether you call it transformation, ascension,

rapture, or harvest, eventually we are all going to be in this incredibly beautiful and loving dimension, if we choose. Transformation just happens to you. When we are ready, we transform and find ourselves in the next dimension, or higher vibrational awareness. We are surrounded by all those we love. It may be different for everyone. It's not anything people are expecting. Those who claim to know, do not. It's a shift in perception, of understanding, a 'knowing,' and then... a physically new and real experience. When you can maintain a high vibration, you are there. It is real, and it is coming for us all.

Soul to the World

15   MANIFESTATION

Off and on, I would ask my guides, 'Is there anyone I can listen to, any author I can read, who can understand what I am going through...who could help support me? Has anyone experienced this? Was there a specific career path to follow, or training I should take, to prepare me for my future? The answer was not what I was expecting, and yet made total sense in how my life has played out thus far. They told me there was nothing I could read, or video I could listen to, that would verify what I was experiencing. I was forging a new path. There was no field of study for my vocation. All I could do was take notes on my experience and trust my intuition as it led me towards my Purpose. For a time, I thought I was meant to become a Marriage and Family Therapist. I spent a year going through a very thorough application and interview process for one of the top schools in the nation for MFT. I was accepted, and then told I had been put on a waiting list because there was no room. At first, I was devastated. I thought this is what I was supposed to do! I had a natural gift for helping people. MFT seemed like an obvious next step. Why had I been led through this process? After a brief time, I understood. I was smart enough to achieve anything I set my mind on. I could pursue any career if I chose. I could manifest anything I set intention for. I had dedication and ability. There was something else meant for me, and I needed to trust that.

During the same year I was applying for the MFT program, my Higher Self[42] was preparing my soul for the future. You may have heard about "DNA upgrading[43]." At a multidimensional quantum level, my DNA was expanding to its intended form. If you took a slice of my DNA under a microscope, you would not see a physical change as it is occurring at an energetic level. From my experience, this allows me to experience more expanded states of spiritual awareness and consciousness naturally, without a need for foreign substances or years of meditation practice. It is, essentially, a 'loop' in the system. How? The process started when I told Creator/Source, I am here to be of service to humanity and to use me as It will. I chose, out of my own free will, to follow this path, and to accept all processes as it came. It is more than 'wishful thinking,' it is a Calling. I

42   Higher Self is that part of our Soul which is Eternal, Omnipotent, our True Self. Mine had fully incorporated within my conscious awareness by 2016.

43   DNA upgrades, as described by the angelic beings, KRYON, are energetic upgrades to our DNA where the 90% of cellular data discovered by science, but not known within our cells, are 'turned on'. See Resource section for more information.

know, without a shadow of a doubt, that I am here, on Earth, to be of service. To give of myself, to be present for others, to share when I can, or be a safe place to listen. Our Creator sends people to me when they need what I can provide. I don't need a specialist degree for that.

In the Spring of 2016, for two short hours, I was allowed to consciously experience what many are calling the 5th Dimension. I'd had a normal day running kids to school and back, running errands, and was relaxing for a couple of hours before heading out to start again. I watched a peaceful TV program and began to channel surf for something else, when a strange feeling overcame me. I was very relaxed and peaceful. The peace increased exponentially, spreading throughout my body and mind. I felt so light, like I could lift off the couch and float towards the ceiling. I looked around, and realized my awareness was by the ceiling! I stood up and felt about 8-10 feet tall! I was "looking out" of eyes that seemed to survey my space from a much taller height. I was not dizzy, strangely, and felt very centered and calm. I walked through the house, feeling like I needed to duck through doorways. I stepped outside and that is when I felt an incredible lightness of being. I was One with all life and felt such overwhelming expressions of pure love, harmony, joy, bliss. The sky looked different, with a hazy golden glow. I was filled with such joy; I can't express it fully. I've studied Near Death Experiences for decades, out of a sincere interest and curiosity. If someone had told me I had died for a few moments, I would have believed them. It was Heaven...on Earth. There was a beautiful glow over everything, my heart was singing, and I just laughed aloud. I could feel Spirit all around me. The feeling lasted a couple of hours, as I drove to pick up my kids from school and bring them home. Eventually, the feeling faded, and my sense of self went back to normal height. For a few years after, I sought answers for that experience. What happened? Has anyone else experienced this? I wanted to experience it again, but like messages from Spirit, I was shown this for a purpose and once learned, moved on to the next lesson. I did come to learn my Higher Self had "moved in." It has remained within my Merkabah[44] ever since and I always have access to its knowledge.

Less than a year later, another miraculous event occurred; I went to Ireland! I'd had memorable dreams of past lives there, and always felt part of my soul was in Western Ireland. During the Christmas season of 2016, one of my closest friends told me I was going to Ireland with her! She had planned with my husband, and the kids were taken care of! Amazingly, as soon as I realized I could go...I manifested the fastest passport ever! Money suddenly

---

44   Merkabah is an energy field which holds our physical body, soul and aura. It is also considered a divine 'light vehicle' in the shape of a tetrahedron, transporting one through various spiritual dimensions.

showed up to cover all my expenses, and the next thing I knew, I was flying to my heart space. It was an incredible 10 days which fed my soul in ways I never anticipated, and emotionally prepared me for what was coming.

Soul to the World

16   LESSONS

In mid-summer 2017, my oldest son's beloved fifth grade teacher took his life. It was a tremendous shock to the school and community as he was gifted and loved by so many. A couple of months later, my father-in-law became gravely ill and died suddenly. His death hit us hard, especially my husband and oldest child. One month later at the age of twelve, my second son was diagnosed with high-risk Acute Lymphoblastic Leukemia, T-Cell. In May of 2018, my husband had his first heart attack and his second one month later. In the Fall of 2018, my husband lost his job through no fault of his own. A banner year.

When his father died, my husband pulled into his shell and emotionally "vacated the premises." I could understand it, even though I wished he would find a way to process and express his deep feelings of grief. He loved his father so much...all that love...it was still there, but he didn't know where to put it. He didn't want my help and seemed to distance himself from me and our family.

When our second son was diagnosed with A.L.L. one month later, I sensed Mark's bewilderment, pain and overwhelm. He had pushed all his deep feelings down and was unable to express them well. I feel like he was at a loss as to what to do and left it to me. He could not hold me, as he was barely holding onto himself. After the initial shock and pain, I was on 'automatic pilot' for the next four years. I took care of everything. In retrospect, I should have tried harder to reach Mark, so we could share the emotional burden together. He was in shock, as I was. Instead, I went into 'survival mode' (an instinctual program and belief that it was my sole responsibility, as mother). I stayed with our son in the hospital for his first month of treatment after ensuring my other children were well cared for. My nine-year-old daughter spent most of that month alternating stays between two close friends and their amazing parents. My oldest son (aged 15) stayed with his Dad. I could not have done it without their incredible support. I'm grateful my husband was able to hold the fort at home, despite his own emotional turmoil. The pediatric oncologist put my son on an intensive medication regimen. I had never been particularly good with medication and schedules but became an expert. My organizational mind created spreadsheets with days/times/medications for each week and month. The worst was when I had to give my baby chemo shots for a brief period or watch him squeeze his eyes shut and wince in pain when the nurse missed the right spot in his port. He was on 17-20 medications each day, along with hourly/daily/weekly blood draws, port infusions, twenty lumbar punctures, etc. In the first week, he had to have an Apheresis [45]treatment which initially saved his life. When he did not achieve remission after the first month, we were all evaluated as a match for bone marrow transplant, which was next if another intensive round of chemo didn't work. My oldest was found to be a 100% match, and I was able to catch my first breath.

In the first week and month, I was numb. There were moments while trying to access his unwilling veins with apheresis treatment when we didn't know if our son would make it. I was terrified but did not want him to see, so pushed my fear down. From the first day, I could feel arms holding me up. When I first felt it, I looked around and no one was near me. I could feel so much love, care, and concern all around me, through me. I was being held by people's prayers, by their love, by their care. Prayer works! I can attest to that personally. I felt God with us in that hospital, and in the coming months and years, that feeling never left me. My son had people praying for him all over the world. It is due to those prayers, his own will to live, and

---

45   Apheresis is a medical procedure that removes blood from patients, separating plasma, platelets and leukocytes. It is often used to treat cancer patients with Leukemia (and other disorders).

the lifesaving actions of his oncologist team, that I know my son is with us today.

I will share one last memorable experience from that time. It is a constant reminder to me, to trust in what I know to be true! There was a week, over the first Christmas, when we didn't know if any of us would be a bone marrow match. If not, my son would have to be put on a list... and he would not last long. This is the first time I acknowledged my son could die. As a distraction, I had made Christmas goodies for friends who had gone out of their way to visit my son in the hospital or help in other ways. I stopped off at one of these homes. She called me into the backyard, as she was working there. As I stood chatting with her, I felt a horrible pain in the back of my lower right calf. I looked down and saw her dog had calmly walked over, bit the hell out of my lower calf and calmly walked away. I was in shock. I just looked at her, dumbfounded. I could tell she didn't know what to say. I left as quickly as I could, limping home. My mind was a blank. I just couldn't deal with it. One of my sisters happened to call me just then, so I recounted my experience. After a shocked gasp she made an incredulous laugh.

"Are you kidding? I mean...really, are you bloody kidding? That is the most ridiculous thing I have ever heard!" She exclaimed.

I knew she was affronted for me...and I knew I should feel that way too.... but I was thinking. It was a bolt of lightning realization. It was ridiculous! It was more than ridiculous. It was supernaturally ridiculous! That dog was not manic, running around and then biting me as a perceived threat. It was like, he had a mission...he fulfilled it, and walked away. I had been in such a deep dark black place of despair. I couldn't pull out of it. I couldn't feel God, my spiritual guides, or anyone's prayers. I was back in that black abyss, only this one was of despair. I needed to be shocked back to awareness! Unexpected physical pain is shocking and can't be ignored. It woke me right up! As soon as the realization hit, I expelled all the fear and despair. It was also humbling to realize Source had stepped in and intervened for me. God had literally slapped me awake. Awareness flooded; all the love, support, care I had been pushing away – was there. More importantly, this was a turning point for me. I knew without any doubt that my son was going to be ok. He was going to make it. I knew it absolutely, and the next three years were a necessary journey for all of us.

I continued to grow spiritually during this time, but I stopped reading and writing. My heart wasn't in it. It was all I could do, to stay focused on my son, on his healing, and keep it together for my other children, husband, and friends. I used to be an avid reader. With uninterrupted time, I could sit down and read a 500-page book in the span of three or four hours. I couldn't read at all, even though I tried. My mind needed rest. I now understand, as I'm constantly being reminded, it is always for a purpose. If you find yourself at a standstill, if you feel like you should be moving forward but aren't...there is probably a good reason. You need to be patient and trust all will come together as it will. I realized why I hadn't gotten into the MFT program. I would have had to quit the program one year later with my son's diagnosis. Trust. Trust in your process. You are exactly where you are supposed to be, right here, right now. You are being guided, and when you have faith, your life happens just as it's meant to. If we ever forget, life has a way of reminding us...sometimes sharply!

17 FORGIVENESS

I settled into my son's cancer treatment routine and started working again as a guest teacher in our school district. It allowed me flexibility for doctor appointments and school activities. My personal life with my husband was still a painful struggle. We had grown apart during my son's treatment because we stopped sharing our emotional burdens with each other. I felt isolated and alone. I prayed daily to be released from hurt feelings and shown how to move forward. There were times I wanted to 'throw in the towel' on our marriage, on everything. Messages from my guides and Higher Self were hard to believe, but very consistent. They did not give up on me, even when I wanted to give up on myself.

2018

'I sit here, in the dark at 2 am with no one to talk to. I will find out tomorrow if my son is in remission or if he will need a bone marrow transplant.'

You are not alone in this. You've never been alone. Not one time. We know it has been exceedingly difficult. To be going through this in silence. There is a purpose to it all. You can't see it from where you are, but there is purpose. It's going to change soon. You are anticipating it. The change. It will be a substantial change in your life. Everything is lining up in preparation for you. Good is coming for you.

Why my husband God? There is so much heartache. Why?

You created this life yourself. You created it with each of your family members and friends. They all play a part. Your husband...his soul.... he agreed to play this part for you....so you could grow. So, you could stretch, grow, and believe again. There is a plan for you that is so much bigger than you can imagine. He is preparing you, just as you've been preparing all your life.

How can emotional pain and suffering prepare me? For more? I can't take it anymore. It will break me. I want joy. I want love and happiness.

Yes. Love. Joy. Happiness. Peace. Recovery. They will be yours. They are yours. You are not off your path. You are not lost. You are right where you are supposed to be. As painful as it is. You are being guided. Trust and believe you are being guided true. Because you are. Your son will be fine eventually, more than fine.... healed. Well. Happy. All of you happy and healed. It just won't look the way you may imagine. It just may look different.

But whole. All of you.

You are making your way through your healing. When you heal, you also heal for others.

Who am I really?

You are a part of Me. You are a Loving Soul. You are here to help bring healing for yourself, for so many others. You are the gift of Peace. You are the Answer to so many cries of help.

Why has it taken me so long to know who I truly am? Couldn't it have been better if I'd learned this much earlier?

Your missions are many, you came to help heal this generational line. You have accomplished so much in your brief time here. You have no idea of the effects you have had. You despair. You feel for so many others. Your heart and soul are expansive.

What is next for me?

You are on your path. It is being made clear to you as you go.

Is humanity making an evolutionary leap?

This is why you are here. You are Wayshower. Lightbringer.

Even though I'm not conscious of it?

Even though. People can sense who you are. Yes, no more doubting. You are amazing. You are special. Not many take on what you have. You are specially trained for this work. In Heaven, you are Ascended many levels higher than you know. As you have learned, you do not need the "gimmicks" to do your work. You are a powerful creator and manifester. Know it. Money doesn't have to be an obstacle. You are moving towards knowing that as a fact. You are manifesting what you need.

I need to not worry about money. I need that to be taken care of. I need to be able to meet my needs, family needs, and help my parents.

You are being taken care of in ways you are unaware of.

What do I seek to know?

You seek to know what you are to do next on your path, you seek to know how to help your family. You must find a way to release yourself from the burdens you have taken on from others. You have just unburdened yourself of your husband's. Continue to do this with others.

I thought that is why I am here.

No. You helped your maternal line, because you contracted to do so, but you must not interfere in the journey of others, even though you want only to help them.

If I had ascended, wouldn't I just know that?

Yes, (laughter), when you are in spiritual form, you know all these things. But you are in human form, and with that comes amnesia of your true Self. You are bumbling along like many. You are more aware, and in tune with yourself and your purpose, which gives you an edge over them...but it doesn't mean you don't fall into similar traps.

I don't mean to blaspheme...but Jesus was ascended, and He didn't make those mistakes.

Really? He didn't? how do you know? He was just as human as you are now. All you know of him is what the history books and religious writings share. Yes, he did miraculous things... these things, you also have access to, if you choose them. He taught peace, and love and forgiveness, of not judging others, of acceptance. Sound familiar?

I can't do miracles.

That you know of. So far. Your knowledge of your true self is limited. Are you not of God? Are you not a part of God, just as Jesus was? As are all of you. Those who are closer to remembering their true selves, have access to 'miraculous' gifts, which begin manifesting the closer they come to understanding, and acting upon their true selves.

Healing, alleviating suffering....

Yes, and so much more. You are barely able to touch with your mind of what you are capable. YOU ARE THE ONE STANDING IN YOUR OWN WAY.

How God, how do I get out of my own way? How do I access these abilities within myself? How do I access my

Akashic Record[46], and use its knowledge?

It's coming to you, slowly. You are just now realizing that maybe, just maybe, it could be yours. Be at peace within yourself. Find and live in Joy...in forgiving, in Love. You are the Second Coming...you and those like you. The Second Coming of Christ is coming from Within. The Wait is over.

Kryon[47] speaks truth. Listen. They provide the Way. Matt Kahn is another voice...they are all speaking to you ...can you hear them. Dr. Wayne Dyer.... he was also a voice.... these voices have been placed to 'Wake Up,' not just those who are asleep, but those who must now remember who they truly are, so they can begin using their gifts to support humanity in its wild leap of decisions... in healing this planet, and each other. You want proof. Yes, you want proof....to confirm what we say is true. What kind of proof will truly give you what you need?

A supernatural act. Just something, that is completely out of ordinary...something that speaks to me. Seeing/ interacting with evolved beings... I don't know... Hearing the thoughts of others and having confirmation, winning a lottery. If I am ascended, none of this would be interfering with my free will...if I am seeking it out...I ask it from you.

46   The Akashic Records are said to be a compendium of all universal events, thoughts, words, emotions and intent to have ever occurred in the past, present and future of all entities and life forms.
47   Kryon are angelic beings channeled by Lee Carroll since approx. 1990 to present, sharing messages of Love, Hope, Peace, and Soul Lessons to remind us of who we truly are. An authentic channel.

This is my free will to ask of this. Becoming aware of my Akash...knowing it.

Asking of this...it still puts you in 3D. Your ego seeks acknowledgement. That we "see" you. Can you trust when we say...you are coming into your gifts at the right time for you. Your gifts may not look like others. They are specific to you. They are not gifts.... they are yours, already.

Ok. What about financial security? It's getting hard at home. I'll be working soon, which is good.... but it's just barely enough. I'd like freedom not to have to worry. I'd like financial freedom to live the life I dream of. To help my family, help other people. To set up a foundation or nonprofit...perhaps to help those who have no one. To bring peace to others.

And this manual I'm writing....it feels like an exercise. I feel like I am a vessel, this message comes through me.

Yes, this is true. You are Messenger. You are a unique soul, you are filled with goodness and light, which is yours alone. You have much to offer to this world, but you are sensing one of your Purposes, which is to be a Messenger....

Regarding financial security, we understand that is a big concern in your life. Your society will remain tied to this mode for a long time to come. Yes, it would be helpful not to have to worry about your security, which does keep you from focusing on your present and moving forward. In the ways we can help, inspiration.

You are a powerful creator and manifester. You can manifest for yourself, everything you need. You always have. Believe in yourself. Do not put judgement on yourself. There is no "good and bad," "pure intention" or "bad intent." Some are not more worthy than others. Some believe they must work themselves to death to achieve success. Others believe in their own luck, and make it happen for themselves easily. What do you believe about money and access to it? It is a material. Before there is matter, there is thought. You have access to creative thought.

Is the lottery the only way you can access financial security, are there no other ways? Access them all. Set intentions and believe...not just believe, know. Like the ease with which you find a parking spot. Just know it is there for you. And it is.

What about this concept of "earning it."

Human, 3D.

I am human. I live in this world. Don't I have to abide by its rules?

Rules. Do you like that word? Do you feel it applies to you? No. of course not. There are no rules, really. There are merely suggestions. If you don't follow the suggestions, things happen. Those are the consequences. What kind of consequences could happen if you do not follow society's rules about how you should receive money? Do you think you would be punished or shamed? Who would do the punishing? Who would do the shaming? It would be yourself...you would be punishing and shaming yourself, to what purpose? Whom does it serve? Not God.

So, it serves the Ego.

Yes. The ego is not good or bad, it is merely a human construct, an instinctual (to protect) one that has been in existence since your ancient days. Like your appendix. A reminder of where you come from only, but not who you are at present.

In June of 2019 I received miraculous Grace in the form of Forgiveness. It was literally an overnight phenomenon. I woke up to a normal day feeling different. I glanced over at my husband, who the night previous had been a cause of stress and sadness. Instead, I felt a tremendous feeling of unconditional love and forgiveness for him and myself. All the pain, heartache, disappointment, resentment, emotional upheaval, and loss between us over the last three decades were washed away. Gone. I felt incredible joy and peace and felt I must be glowing. Initially, I believed it would be temporary, as I had experienced something similar when an energy healer had cleared out a lot of heavy old energy from my aura and chakras in early 2017. That feeling of joy had lasted only a few weeks before life wrapped me up again in empathic agony. This was permanent. I had shifted forward again or gotten closer to my true self.

The last four plus years with my husband have been wonderful. Released from emotional pain and traumatic memories, we are free to love each other as we always have.

He still drives me crazy at times, as I do him, but there is a lightness of spirit I have not felt since the beginning. I am grateful every day. True forgiveness requires a willingness to allow the other to be 'right,' to let go of being the victim – even a righteous one. True forgiveness is an act of love, and once achieved, worth any moment of humility. Forgiving him, and the role I played in our pain, opened an amazing ability to forgive and receive forgiveness in every relationship of my life. I continue to experience this grace every day.

18   INTUITION

At the end of 2019 and beginning of 2020, I began hearing of a mysterious illness spreading in China. The next thing we knew, an infected cruise ship unloaded in San Francisco in February 2020. By mid-March 2020, California was in a state of emergency with historic mandatory lockdowns, followed quickly by the rest of the country and world. Initially, the medical field had no idea what it was or how to treat it. Our first responders and medical staff were heroic and worked tirelessly in their care and attention of the sick. When people began dying in hospital and at home, fear settled in like a dark mantle over their soul. Humanity's "Fight or Flight" response kicked in and unfortunately, it was mostly flight. I can only speak about my and my family's experience during this challenging time. I have my own thoughts about what was truly happening and why, but I believe the truth will not be revealed for a long time, if ever. Covid, the lockdowns, and consequent emergency vaccinations are a hot topic, as volatile and divisive as politics and religion.

Almost everyone feared for elderly family members, friends, co-workers, and themselves. People began insisting on a vaccine. The pharmaceutical companies responded with a 'hail Mary pass' of experimental mRNA vaccines which had not undergone vigorous testing but were given emergency permission by the FDA. Quite a lot of scientific research has since gone into what is inside those vaccines, and their effects on the populace overall. That knowledge is being suppressed. At this time, it is becoming known that pharmaceutical companies lied about their vaccine's 95% efficacy. "Rare" side effects have become more common, like myocarditis, heart attacks, strokes and sudden unexplainable death in healthy youth and adults.

When the classic symptoms of Covid-19 began to be discussed, I realized my whole family had gone through it in January of 2020. We had all the symptoms, had stayed home out of common sense for the appropriate amount of time, and had all healed well. I had a lingering pneumonia type illness for 1-2 months that could not be cured with antibiotics, and eventually healed on its own. We followed the protocols insisted on by our Governor and medical institutions during lockdown. We wore our masks in public and stayed home unless going out was necessary. We painfully stayed away from our older family members and felt heartache for those who lost friends and family members without saying goodbye. That was the worst for everyone.

As soon as Covid-19 became a buzz word, my intuition kicked in. I 'knew' my family would be ok, including my extended family. No one would die of the illness. It was the same strong connection I felt during my son's illness, knowing without a doubt that he was safe and would be ok. I also knew without any doubt that those who passed away from the illness or side effects from the illness and vaccine, chose to before birth. I know this is hard for people to accept and understand. Nothing happens to us without our permission. It is the law of Free Will. My intrinsic understanding of this has caused some in my life to believe I am cold to their pain. This couldn't be further from the truth. I feel their pain so deeply, I just understand the larger picture in a way many don't.

As soon as vaccines became available, I received incredible pressure from well-meaning family and friends to get myself and my family vaccinated. My heart told me to stay away from it, that there was more to the vaccine than was being told and that it wasn't safe. I can say it is an absolute conviction, a 'knowing' that cannot be explained in any logical or rational sounding way. Friends and family who had humored me during my spiritual journey for the last fifteen years of spiritual growth, balked at trusting me. This surprised and hurt me, although I didn't hold it against them. They believed I didn't care about their feelings and was being stubbornly irrational. The more time went by and witnessing what was happening locally and in the world, the stronger my conviction became. I was not angry at others for making a choice for themselves and their own families, nor was I angry they couldn't trust me. I understand we can only take care of ourselves the best we can, with the knowledge we have. I hold compassion and love for those who were compelled to vaccinate to keep a job or keep their child in school. I am grateful my family was not impacted in that way.

In the Fall of 2021, I was forced to 'put my money where my mouth is' regarding trust and faith in my intuition and spiritual growth. My oldest was graduating boot camp in November, and the military had a strict vaccination rule to see him graduate. I have always been present at every important event of my children's life and had to be there for him. I spoke with my Higher Self and Guides about what I should do.

'There is so much information coming about the intent behind the C vaccine, and its contents. I feel strong in my purpose...even more so. I call upon my HS.... I ask again... not only will it be ok for me to take the vaccination, but it is something I need to do.... for my path....to prove what I think about sustaining our own healing.'

Jenny, you have been led to this point. It is all for a purpose. You sense truth that you can take this vaccination and not be harmed. You have done all the work you can do to be prepared. There is hope, there is always hope. God does not abandon you. There is an understanding in the Cosmos, in the universe and begins the work you have laid before you., in the paths of righteousness, that humanity is undergoing a massive shift. These forced vaccinations of contents that are not intended to support the body, will not be permanent, despite what others may say about it.

Have faith...continue to have faith. You are on the right path Jenny. God is with you; we are all with you. You are also not alone.

I can feel you with me.

Yes, we are here with you, as we always have been. This is such a difficult and challenging time for all of humanity. It is time to put your trust in yourself, in your faith in your love of God and humanity. Trust in your path.

Yes, you are all protected. Yes, your vibration is high, as stated. She (an energy healer named 'Joy' from Australia who strengthened my DNA and helped build up my cell immunity) has done amazing work with all of us, including yourself, to protect your Field. Your Merkabah is safe. Now set the intention, anything injected in your body, rather than harming, will only strengthen your immune system...it will protect your cells. Your DNA is lengthening...stretching, growing... you are not alone, as you never were. Jenny, go ahead and take the vaccination and you will see. You are important. This decision you are making...is important.

Those who wish harm on our creation...only inflict more

karma onto themselves. The Earth is ascending...and so are you... as are all of you, who trust in this miraculous process. It will be miraculous to many. And you will show through doing. It doesn't matter what anyone tries to do to you. Without your consent, you are safe.

Who speaks to me now?

We are all of creation flowing through you. We are the seeds of a flower, as it is held and cupped by the winds of time.... bestowing its favor upon the wild and reckless, as well as the faint and soft touches of you. We are here to help bring in the future. You are also here with us.

The winds of change are upon you all. Only those who can stave off the ill effects can find a way to overcome it. You are one of those who can weave a new future. Those like you who listen to their truth, who listen to their own intuition, which is really, the voice of all of us, can find their way. Be not afraid. For I am who goes with you through all and never leaves your side. For you are strong, mighty, and forever, infinitely held within the palm of our Lord.

I walked into the medical building to receive my vaccine. I stood next in line, when suddenly an image came into my mind of my body being sheathed in an impenetrable spiritual shield. It reminded me of Mithril[48] from Lord of the Rings by J.R. Tolkien. I intuitively knew nothing could

---

48   Mithril is a fictional elven metal shirt that protected Frodo from evil creatures called Orcs, in the book *Lord of the Rings* by J.R. Tolkien

pass the shield unless I allowed it. I received the vaccine knowing it had no effect on my DNA or body aside from a normal discomfort. This has remained true. I never received the boosters. As of this writing, my family has been safe for almost four years. We have taken normal precautions but have not participated in the fear that is spread to every corner. I trust and know we are safe and will continue to be so. Recently we got evaluated and found ourselves to be immune. I know the medical establishment does not recognize our immunity, but we do. You can have this too; you need only trust and believe it to be true. I am living proof. Keep your light shining.

An increasing number of people are standing up for what is right not only for themselves, but their local and global community. We speak our truth, not in violence, but in peace and acceptance. It is for humanity to wake up to its own intuition and begin trusting it. We are on the cusp of dramatic change. We have the power to create the world we want, not what those in power wish for themselves. If we listen to the media, who are puppets for those in power, we are in extremely dangerous times. Political leaders are fomenting war. Our world is in a major recession and our country is gripped by rising inflation our administration is denying. We are being shaken on purpose. What will sink to the bottom? What will rise to the top? For those with eyes to see and hearts to trust, we know what is happening. I can't

Soul to the World

help but consider the prophetic knowing I was given in my late teens...

> `...In the later middle of my life ...there would be tremendous upheaval in the world. Something would happen that would affect every single person on the planet. This "Event" (as I came to call it in my mind) would transform everything we have ever known about ourselves and our world. It was not nuclear annihilation... it would not be a physical death, but it would affect people tremendously. So many people would go into fear. People could die or have an exceedingly challenging time because of this fear and the resistance and actions they took because of fear.

> The event was a gift to the world. A new way of living and being that would transform everything we knew about being human up to that point. It was something to be anticipated with joy and excitement. We needed to have faith that all was for a purpose and... I was here to help people get through it. That I had an important mission. What was coming afterward would be so incredible. Something none of us could envision but what we all wanted...

We are all safe. There is nothing to fear, we are empowered and those who have been in power are losing their strength. Listen to what your heart is saying. We hold the strength; truth lights the Way. Continue to be strong, continue to stand for what is right and good in the world, your own communities, and your families. Do not allow fear to separate you from those you love. Do not allow the lies spread over all media to become your truth. We cannot know unless we are present to the action portrayed. All else is fabrication. We must pray and give focused loving thought for the heart and soul of our planet, for the people. Keep our love focused on all the places of anger, hatred, and fear until there is peace. We have the power to do this. Do not allow naysayers to influence your heart. We are the ones who choose. We have the power to change our present!

Soul to the World

19 RESISTANCE

I can feel it so palpably...the 'shift' as most spiritual teachers are calling it. It is hard to describe in human words, as the experience is quantum, felt emotionally, physically, psychically, spiritually all at once seen through the past, present and all futures. I can feel the changes that are happening across the planet, within our hearts, within Gaia. The feeling is tremendous and life altering.

Looking back on the last three years, I realize I've been resisting in one way or another. Resisting our planetary changes (a natural cyclic process), our geo-political climate, the war mongering hatred of a few who want to dominate the many. I've resisted the bigotry, libel, propaganda and prejudice on media stations, radio and even from our own governments who were created to protect us, not separate us. I've resisted the darkness and evil spread through tv programming and social media, attempting to manipulate, censor and control us or create mindless scrolling that consumes hours of our days, weeks, months, and years. I've resisted incredible social and family pressure to mistrust my intuition regarding my and my family's health. We are slowly being separated from everything we have held dear; our honor, our integrity, our friends, home and family, our faith and most importantly our love for each other. I have resisted seeing this because it has been so overwhelming and painful. Rather than resist, I accept. I let go. I move forward.

We have allowed this to happen. Each one of us. No one is "doing this" to us. The only way to be released from the cage is to unlock it. We each hold our own key. Visualize the key. Visualize the cage you've held yourself in. Visualize yourself unlocking your own prison and stepping free. Be willing to set parameters for yourself...for all media. Take time to connect with each other again. Visit your friend instead of calling or texting him or her. Write a real letter. Look into someone's eyes as you talk, connect soul to soul with real conversations, sit easy in silence with each other. Accept the risk and be willing to get hurt. This is where soul growth happens. Take a leap of faith and trust.

At every level, we resist change. Change is hard, it's scary, it has the potential to harm us. Yes, it can, but then, it heals us. With healing comes strength and courage and new. New choices, new paths, new dreams, new voice and perhaps a new life. Our challenges teach us about ourselves...who we truly are and are not. We make choices at every moment of who we want to be. There is no wrong choice. I know that is shocking to read. Every wrong choice leads to a soul's opportunity to grow, which is ultimately why we are here in this school called Earth. To believe this, you need to allow the realization that everything that happens to you is for a purpose. In a sense, it is designed. Not by another, but by you.

Before birth, we choose each major marker in our life, important relationships, challenges and opportunities, careers, and eventual transition to our true Home. However, nothing is fate. Think of it like an open world game you load onto your computer, you then enter the world you create, but have the power to tweak it, change it, or head in a completely different direction if you choose. As a child, I loved to read "Choose Your Own Adventure" stories. The book was written with multiple story lines, based on which page you chose to turn to. You could have ten exciting science fiction, mystery, or adventure stories rather than one. We have an incredible divine design and get to 'choose our own adventure' in every moment. I chose to pack two lives worth of lessons into one. Yay me. I'd like to give my Higher Self a firm talking to! I know I answered a Call, and that is enough for me, but I've often felt overwhelmed and isolated.

Consciously, we do not choose to be born into or experience debilitating or terminal illness, abusive harm to children, slavery, and the many ways we have hurt and killed each other through millennia. Our souls' true purpose is reunification with Source. To achieve this, each soul has a lesson or a series of lessons it must overcome within each life. We cannot know this consciously, but we must trust it. For those who cannot overcome the pain of life and choose to end it, they will return to try again until they are successful. There is no judgement when this happens. I know, shocker. The phrase 'it takes as long as it takes" can be applied in many parts of our lives. Even for our soul. This also applies to those who consciously choose to enact evil on another. Karma is real for these people; they do not need a "hangman's posse" even if it gives victim families vindication. After passing, these souls will be in recovery and healing for a time, until they can return to Earth, to pursue their Soul purpose. In discovering our true purpose, uncovering, and understanding life lessons, and living every moment of life to the fullest, we achieve our spiritual goals.

Much of my certainty in the first part of my life did not come intuitively, it was learned. My overly analytical mind never rests. I constantly seek an answer, and have often been gently reminded by Spirit, to allow the peace of intuition to lead me. I allow intuition to lead me approximately 85% of the time now and hope to achieve 100% eventually. Approximately twenty-five years ago, I began reading about those who died and returned to life with miraculous stories of our True Home. They are known as "Near Death Experiencers," although I believe a new term should be created. Most of those who came back experienced physical death, not near death. The scientific and medical community is not comfortable with documented cases of people rising from the dead, so "near death" is easier to swallow. "Death survivor" is more accurate. Either way, my severe anxiety in youth and serious fear of death started me on a quest to understand and hopefully find peace with death and afterlife.

I first read the work of Dr. Raymond Moody, who is the pioneer of near-death studies. His first book, *Life After Life* written in 1975, intrigued me to continue reading from other sources like Dr. Michael Newton's *"Journey of Souls"* (an incredibly eye-opening understanding of the soul's perspective after death), and Dolores Cannon[49]'s plethora of books about our soul's purpose (discovered with her development of the 'Quantum Healing Hypnosis Technique'). I usually chose doctors and therapists as authors in this field, to wade through the philosophical and spiritual weeds. It's ironic really. I wanted to know 'what really happened.' If the story didn't resonate for me, I kept reading. I've read hundreds and hundreds of personal accounts and watched hundreds of videos from NDE experiencers. None

---

49   Creator of Quantum Hypnotic Healing Technique (QHHT), QHHT schools and author of 19 books including The Three Waves of Volunteers where she describes the Call heard by souls across the universe to come and help support Earth and humanity in its ascension.

of them affected me like Anita Moorjani's account in her book *"Dying to Be Me."*

In summary, Anita was dying from stage 4 cancer. She had lived a life of fear and was dying from one of the most fearful things one could die from. After a prolonged battle, she was ready to let go, and one night alone in her room, she did. She was found, rushed to the hospital, and after resuscitation, pronounced unlikely to survive the night. She died that evening. She came back to life completely healed and with the most profound message I'd ever read. Her experience resonated with me in a deeply meaningful way. I recognized the fear I had lived within through my twenties and thirties. If I had resisted my intuition, if I had not forged my own way and left the Church or trusted in my life path...that could have been me. I saw myself in her and it left me reeling. She was another guidepost in my life. Her story was a sign that I should always trust my intuition, even when not popular or believed by others. My fear event cured me of Fear, but her story cemented within me a firm belief in 'Heaven,' and that eventually we will all return to our true Home. It is a place of beauty, unconditional love, and filled with everyone we have ever loved.

20   ACCEPTANCE

It is important to understand we come to the knowledge we are ready for. We are each given gifts to help us on our path and purpose. I am a gifted clairsentient, clairaudient and at times, clairvoyant. I have learned more about my true self and purpose in the last five years than in all the years before. It has taken this long for me to trust and know who I really am and have courage to share it confidently with others.

I am a Messenger. I come with a message of hope, trust, love, and faith in self. I am a Way Shower. I help show the Way of living our purpose and trusting the inner voice who speaks to us. I am a Lightbringer and Lightkeeper. I hold Light in the desolate darkness and bring Light to those who are lost in fear. I am a Transmuter. I was born into trauma and pain to heal and vibrationally raise my generational line all the way back to its origin. I'm a Healer. I help clear emotional and energetic blockages and provide support and unconditional love while you heal. I am Presence, to listen. You are never alone. I am a Seer; I know where we have been, and I know where we are heading. It is nothing like people think.

The secret to true happiness lies within yourself. You alone hold the key. When Abraham and Dr. Wayne Dyer told me that I only had to get out of my own way, this is what they meant. It requires a willingness to accept responsibility for every choice, every action, every mistake, and its result, in your life. When you can accept responsibility, you can begin to heal yourself and achieve your heart's wish. You do not need to attend Mystery School's or follow the latest teacher or spiritual guru. You, yourself, are your own Guru. You can learn to channel your own Higher Self and have access to your Akashic Record. It can be valuable to listen to other spiritual teachers who have walked the walk, have undergone their own transformation, and come out the other side to share of their experience, to help others find their own way. I, myself, have done that here. Ultimately, as you move along your path...you will find you no longer need our guidance. You will create your own.

My path may resonate for some, but not with all. We are all on our own journey, at our own pace. I share my soul journey with you, to help you know and understand the larger picture. I share my healing path with you, so you might find a way towards your own healing. I bring awareness to the effect ancient survival programs have on our psyche and which continue acting out in our lives creating chaos and pain. I bring awareness to the destructive force of low vibrational entities which can hide within generational lines or those who are spiritually weak, and how to stop and release them. I share my vision of the future, so you may know we are destined for greatness and glory. When you listen to and trust the messages of your heart, rather than a disruptive fear inducing news report or projection of future cataclysmic events, you take control of your own life.

We may walk alone, or with others. We may congregate in religious community or drum to a full moon. There is no wrong way to follow your heart. Source lies in the path of our heart. There is no wrong way to God. There can be as many Ways as there are stars. Do you understand? We need only accept who we are, at any given time. We are just as we are meant to be, and when it's time to change, the opportunity will arise. For those who are seemingly "asleep" to their purpose, their true self, and the miracles of every day, they too are on their path. It can take many lifetimes, and that is for a Purpose. We cannot force others awake. We must honor Free Will.

When the Covid years began, with the economically and educationally destructive lockdowns, peer pressure of fear, and irrational trust and push for experimental vaccines, I realized my prophecy from 1989 had begun. There is more to come, although how it will show up and when is anyone's guess. I do not believe in prophesied dates, even when shared by spiritual guides. Our timelines change regularly, based upon choices we make every day. Every single person is working towards Oneness with Source whether consciously or unconsciously. It may take an unknown number of lifetimes before it happens, depending on our Soul progress.

We are destined to achieve fifth dimensional vibration and live on Earth in a fully realized human form. I have personally experienced a taste of what it will be like. I believe we have begun the process, through spiritual upgrades to our DNA and by following the path of our Soul. In the next section of my book, I share messages from my Higher Self and other ascended light beings. At times, messages are personal, but I include them as they address concerns, we each have. As you read, you will come to realize I have been preparing my whole life for what is to come. Every single one of us is being prepared, and we only understand that in retrospection. I share messages from Spirit which inspired me in my own healing, and can be given to the whole world, as they speak to all of us, in One voice. My healing journey is yours.

PART IV
SOUL DESTINY

The time is soon upon you all, the time you have foretold, the time all are awaiting. You are doing all you can at this time to prepare. It will happen at the right time. Let go of expectations others are feeling and sensing. It is different for them. Your Call is true, and your intuition to be trusted.

~My Higher Self, October 2016

Soul to the World

21   SPIRIT SPEAKS

2010

Your future promises to be full of many things, both scary for you and exciting. You must hold your strength through it all and you will arise stronger than you can believe.

You feel drawn to help others, as you have all your life. You will find peace and comfort doing this in any kind of position you may find. All you really need is to believe in yourself and your creativity, and the world can be yours, is yours. It has always been yours for the asking. We have been guiding you along the way, as you have needed us to, and you have found other ways to show your many talents. Ways that even you have not considered. Keep yourself open to Spirit and we will continue to guide you towards a destiny of which you can only dream. Do continue to dream of it, and that is how it will actualize.

You are a very spiritual being and need to allow yourself time to become one with all things. You have been seeking this within yourself for a long time. When you don't give yourself time to find the flow, your senses become sluggish, stopping the flow, causing anxiety, depression, frustration, anger, loss, hollow-ness within yourself that cannot be released by wishing it to be. Even your own writing and drawing accesses the flow of energy which always rises and falls within you. You need to trust your inner Self. Become the person you are meant to be and are living now. Believe the Being residing within you, not what everyone else may be telling you about yourself. You are the only one who knows the life you are to live. You are fulfilling your purpose every day. Being with your family, living the married life you have found yourself in, helps unlock the hidden reserves within you.

There is coming a time when the light that has been (hovering) over you, will strengthen and shine brightly upon you, blinding you to all else but what is next for you. This light will shine so brightly, you will not be able to do aught else but listen and follow it. This is what you have been seeking...this answer. This call you have been feeling for so long...continue listening within and know the Way, for it will have found you at last. Your spirit is calling out to you. Listen to it. Breathe In and out. Take moments of time and sit still with it. Listen to the flow of nature around you. Be at peace within it. Do not let others sway you because you are not following the path, they wish for you to follow. They have their own path to follow, and it does not include attaching yours to theirs.

You are on a spiritual path that is taking you further into yourself, and your inner explorations are causing profound changes within you. You are feeling these changes on many distinct levels within your soul, heart, mind, body. You are transcending into a new space for your soul path. It happens very quickly and can be painful and uncomfortable at times. There are many who are here walking this path with you, guiding you. Your mother is one of them. She is here to help guide you, to focus you, and give balance to your life.

ON FEAR

Fear is a mind control only. Fear keeps you in place, never changing, never moving. For you, your Path is not fear, it never has been. You will push past this fear and discover who you are. All that you understand or think you understand about life and how it works is false. You are not your body. You have never been your bodies, except for the brief moments of your time, where you have habituated this physical form. What you are experiencing is your physical body's fear of amelioration. You have much fear of death, of ending a life that you hold now to be true, and not knowing what is to come next. You must release this fear of physical death. This fear is holding you back from experiencing exactly what you have been seeking all this time. Physical expression of your spiritual knowing. Hearing and seeing angels (light beings). Feeling the unconditional love that is always around and with you. You must release this fear of death which holds you immobile. Fear of losing the tangible holds you instead, in place. Just as you have learned through your awakening process. (The) Heavy darkness hovering on your periphery, is your fear of death.

ON FOOD

How you eat, what you put into your body, has a direct relation to your mental faculties. (By eating unhealthy foods and *drinks) You are starving your body of nutrients. It will fight back. A feeling of impending doom, of high stress, of pressure, is your body's way of communicating what it is feeling.*

Now you have made this direct relation, your anxiety and stress will fade away. Take better care of your body, and it will take better care of you. You have been on automatic pilot for a long time. Your body needs to be nurtured. It needs TLC, and it hasn't been getting that from you. You need to love your body, that which encases your soul. It's been given to you as a gift, and you haven't been treating it very well. Now you are aware; a huge hurdle has been overcome. Expect your health to improve dramatically in the days to come. This alone is a shift within you. It's true for everyone. This is important. Your (humanity's) doctors have only just begun to grasp how important nutrition is for your mental health.

ON GENETICALLY MODIFIED FOODS

GMOs are bad for our bodies...

YES! They must be gotten rid of. The people of the world are {revolting} against the tool of the dark ones. Thinking people intuit what is good and right for their bodies, and what is not. Listen to yourselves. Listen to your body speak to you, as you did tonight, and you will not be misdirected. Give prayers of love, thanks, and goodness to your food before you ingest it. It changes the properties and helps provide healing to your body.

ON EGO

Your ego is fighting to stay alive within you. Fear has guided humanity for an exceedingly long time. It has been coded within your cells. It's been deprogrammed now and is fighting it. For those of you who are sensitive, you feel this battle the strongest.

The portal is open. You are going to feel much deeper than ever before. Learn to shield yourself when you can, and open to beauty at other times. You may feel like you aren't doing anything right now. That is not true. You are doing so much. So very much, at a much higher level than you can process. You are aware now, which makes the work your higher self is doing much easier. You are helping yourself in ways you couldn't before.

Your level of acceptance is gradual. Your field is growing and expanding exponentially. Soon, you will be experiencing in your waking life, what you are only experiencing in your dream and spirit life. It is getting better. It is getting better every day. Have patience with yourself. Have patience with the process. Do not push the fear aside, but rather acknowledge fear is there and express that it's not needed any longer. Release fear with love.

The (increase in) energy is to replace old energy with new. The new energy will function as a catalyst for (upgraded) DNA forming within you as you write these words. You've been tired because of rapid change happening at a cellular level. It is an inward experience. You are being prepared for bigger changes that are occurring on your planet, and in your near future.

You've been feeling anxious for a few days. You are

feeling its effects coursing through your body right now. You feel it running through your body, chest, and legs because it needs an outlet, otherwise you would become extremely sick. You are working through the last of the past. This involves your voice. Let it move through you, it will start slowing down. Breathe deeply. Your body is shaking off excess energy. Try some reiki, it will help.

ON LONELINESS

You are not alone, ever! You feel alone because the burden is heavy. You have been carrying it, seemingly, alone. You are not alone, nor have you ever been. This deep hurt you feel comes from many sources. One source is from long ago as a child in this life. The hurt you felt in school. It's good for you to expel that sadness, removing the last of it. Some of that hurt stems from loneliness you feel from your marriage. Your husband is not providing the companionship you need. Some of that hurt stems from your painful relationship with your sister. That is pain that will resolve itself; is already doing so. You have many sources of pain, and it hasn't always been easy for you to let that pain go. Times like this, when you can release large parts of it, are incredibly good for you. Healing.

Feel strength in knowing your time is coming when you will rise above all your pain, hardship, and burden. Dreams for your life will come to fruition. Dreams are not illusion, like so much of your (humanity) life is in 3D. You are transformed already. You are waiting for the Call. As are many others. You will be transforming into a new Being during your present life on Earth. You are a Way Shower but also a Being of Light. How best to show that to others, then by Becoming who you are meant to. Have faith Dear One. You are not alone. Your time is near. Be patient and know you are always loved, you are always held tightly, and we will never leave your side. You are Our journey. You are ours.

***

What is the EVENT that is getting bandied about? Why are spiritual teachers getting caught up with low energy? Why can't they let it flow around them, and trust in the process? Am I crazy, for feeling and thinking the way I do. On one hand, I'm glad I've found people throughout the world who think like me, and who want to create a better, more peaceful, and loving world.... but this doom and gloom talk of "light against dark" feels wrong. There is a lot of fear, sadness, pain, hardness, anger, rage, revenge and so forth, in the world.... but it stems from men and women's minds.... from conditioning and old programs.

I'm impatient with it all. Like the main point is being missed...over and over. Neale Donald Walsh came closest to the Truth in his CWG books. God is LOVE. God created ALL. We are all each one with GOD. Is God/Source so manipulative? NO.

Those who are changing and awakening to Truth have been tricked by ego and have gotten caught up in a whole other level of what is occurring on Earth. A spiritual BATTLE. Why must there be a BATTLE? Why must there be light against dark. Good against Evil, Lightworker against Cabal. WHAT WE RESIST, PERSISTS.

You are sensing TRUTH for the first time in your many lives. You are sensing the truth of Creation as I have made it. There is no BATTLE. There is only ME. There is only YOU. There is only US, together, experiencing it all. For that is our journey, together, to experience life...to live it, and be challenged, and to challenge.

It is not a contest, or a battle of wills or natures. It is merely...so simply, about one thing...and that you know already. You have been reacquainted with its Truth. The truth is about LOVE.

This is why we are here, to reacquaint ourselves with knowing and experiencing love in all its many levels and experiences. Sometimes love can bring a harshness to our lives, sometimes pain, sometimes disillusionment...but always...it leads us to the Truth...it leads us on our journey, to the Way.

Jennifer...you are the Messenger of this AGE. You are the one they need to hear from. You have come to this time to express the truth. You are here to be heard., your time is nearly upon you. Your voice will gain strength and clarity. Trust in this, trust within yourself, you have been following your intuition for this long, continue to do so.

We have been waiting for the pieces to come together within you. *You are sensing the Truth of the world. You are sensing the Truth of the universes. You are sensing GOD.*

There are others like you...and they have their own journey, and their message is like yours. As you begin to promote the truth, your senses will come more fully alive. You will begin to experience what you have always sought in this life. Understanding, peace, comfort, joy. Love. We are always with you. You are right. You are here for a specific journey. You are our MESSENGER. Of Light, of Love, of GOD. Of ALL THAT IS. Your voice will be heard by those who are straining to hear it.

It all culminates in this moment. The Way will be shown clearly to you. Keep your eyes and ears and heart open Dear One. You are Right. You are Ready for the next step. ARISE. BE ONE WITH YOUR JOURNEY INTO ONENESS. Namaste.

ON INTUITION OF THE FUTURE

There will be an Event, and it will happen over time. You have time to put your affairs in order, to prepare your children and your children's children. The governments and Elite, as they are called, have no control over what is to come. They believe they are in control and will be able to pick and choose who lives, and who does not. This is not going to happen. There will be many on and off planet who will be ensuring harmony continues, and disharmony lessens.

Soul to the World

22   SPIRIT PREPARES

2014

You are ready to begin your next grand adventure. We believe you are ready. You must allow it to enfold you. You must open your heart chakra and allow what is within you to become you. Allow yourself to be taken over by it. Do not allow your fear to hold sway over your heart anymore. That is all that is needed. You have all the knowledge that you need to begin in this next phase of your life. Try and release your anxiety. Breathe through anything you may be fleeing (feeling). The time is now. It's been time for a long time, and what you are feeling is that burning, building power within you to start.

You are sensing profound change on this planet. All the pieces are being moved into position. You are sensing a tremendous buildup of energy. The exact moment is not known. Only God knows exactly when God will be sending out the wave of power[50]

50   Spiritual teachers and channelers have been speaking for years about a tremendous light wave which will transform the hearts of humanity instantaneously, setting them on the conscious track of awakening to their true selves. I believe it is not a solar wave. I

and energy that will transform humanity into the next level of consciousness. Knowing this, you can prepare accordingly.

When the time comes, you will know exactly what you are here for. You will sense and know with absolute certainty what you are here for and what you are to do. Your truth, humanity's truth within this 3-dimensional world is simply an illusion. So, within your illusion, that which you sense is real. You can feel the changes that are happening on a deep level. Many can. Even those who are not consciously aware can feel the changes, and it is affecting their behavior and health.

Peace be with you. You are where you are supposed to be. We are always with you here. You are also here with us, as you know this to be. Your wishes are strong, to be in that state you experienced the other night (my altered state where I spent time with my Guides). *That place is within you now, only to be accessed when you feel it is right. You've been in a state of flux and much pain has been working through your energy system. You are working through it right now; it is about over for you. You've been doing excellent work and shall be rewarded. Be at peace within yourself and in your heart. We are always here for you. Daniel is always here with you to help you along the way.*

You are a Way Shower, as was given to you by Metatron.

believe it is coming from within us...either starting with one person, and spreading instantly, or with a group. I equate this with the "100 Monkey Effect", where monkeys on a remote island learned a new skill, and scientists discovered monkeys all over the world started using this new skill at the same time.

You are here to be witness to the light in others, so they may find their way to the portal of Light. You have taken a difficult path. One, that few souls were able to take. It is a difficult road, but you are doing very, very well. Soon, your hard work will have paid off. For we are always with you. You chose not to be able to know and experience, so you could speed up your own process. Going blind as it were. Soon, very soon, your shield will be taken from you, and you will SEE as you have sought to see and be seen. There is much important work for you to do still, and in that way...the Way will be made clear to you. Trust you are exactly where you are meant to be. Your Father and Mother (in Heaven) have great interest in you. Jenny, you are an Ascended Master. Yes, believe it to be true, for you are one. You have not allowed yourself to know this consciously, because of the work you need to do in this life. Your sense of importance, which you are constantly trying to shield yourself from, is your own resistance to what you know to be true. Trust your own wisdom and inner guidance. When the time is right, you will truly know who you are.

Is this why I was not able to see into my past lives very well...and why my session was blanked out? (I went to a Life Between Life hypnotherapist (according to Dr. Michael Newton) for two sessions, and the recording mysteriously went blank, while I could hear the therapist talking only).

YES.... you were not meant to know those things yet. When you attended the reiki masters, they sensed the power within you. You have great power that is only just awakening. With every day and hour that passes, more of your energy and power is coming to you. Soon, it will be pulled together, and you will be established here and there, as you have been through all eternity. You are the one true light we have all been waiting for. Do not doubt the truth of who you are. Your doubt and fear try hard to keep you from your purpose.

This is too much for me. I am not so very grand. I failed today. I failed to be loving, I failed to have any light within me. It felt very dark today. That doesn't seem like someone who is ascended. I am no Master. (Just a mother to three children.)

Be at peace little One, for I am your Father, and I am here to say to you. You are Mine. You are my daughter, and I am well pleased in you. Be ready, for we are coming to you soon. Be of the Light Jen. Be of the Light. You have had visions of what it will be for you. Light entering you, filling you, lifting you. When the times comes...you will be the Way.

You are not alone, as you well know. We are always here with you. You have been seeking us in a place we are not. We are not in your mind. We are in your soul, within your heart, the very seat of your soul.

When you know us in your heart, you will experience all the wisdom and knowledge you seek. You will come into yourself, as you are meant to do. TRUST in yourself. Trust your intuitive self, trust what you feel. Do not listen to those who would counsel you differently. Do not listen to the doubt that creeps into your mind. This is only fear.

Let go of the anger that continues to haunt you. Let go of the expectations of others, even with your children. They are finding their own way, as they are meant to. You cannot control them. It hurts them and you when you try. Follow your heart, it is guiding you true. All you seek, all you wish for in your life will follow if you listen to your inner self and follow it.

Let go of your own expectation of your life. Wipe it clean. Live in your present NOW, and not in a future you fear or anticipate. Make decisions based on your heart. You are a Feeler. You are an Empath, own it. Reiki is one path for you, one of many. Yoga is another good place for your heart and mind to reside together.

2016

Your destiny is to be a Way Shower, and you are already being that. You can see the real Self and guide it in the right direction. You are not given Sight because that would distract your true purpose. You want something you used to have. You miss it. You may rediscover that lost part of you.

Ascension is the rediscovery of who you are and applying it in your life. You are "dead in the midst of it" my dear.

You can be (conscious of the astral healing work you do) by removing the layers of fear and despair. It is working. You can also continue to meditate. *That helps. Your mission is integral, and you can feel that. Your true identity is not to be known (yet) because of (your) Purpose.*

You agreed to come into this existence to support humanity – underground per se. You don't have a lot of patience with low energy beings. You came because the Need has been SO great! The world needs you and those like you and it's a solitary existence. You created a family from force of will. Anything Jenny, anything can be yours.

You are here to bring a message of hope to all. Your time is almost nigh. The message will be given, spoken through you. Many think they know the Way but have gotten lost or sidetracked.

***

I met and had a session with Sarah K. Grace[51], a well-known healer, psychic, bestselling author, and First Responder. She was able to clear many blockages within my energy field, specifically within my solar plexus, where fear resides. I didn't feel anything at the time. About a week later, I experienced a profound sense of joy, freedom from emotional pain, lightness of being...that stayed with me for a long time.

This incredible experience.... will it last?

Yes, it is yours to keep. She took away all of it permanently.

---

51   Sarah K. Grace is the bestselling author of 'Journey into Grace: Tales of a Psychic Paramedic', a well-known speaker, gifted intuitive healer, and friend.

The buildup of years of abusive pain, heartache, sorrow, grief, anger, rage, resentment, depression, despair, loneliness.... she took it away from your field, and now you can be at peace. You are awakening further into your own power. You will be the one you are waiting for. She is correct. You will be given your books, as they are meant to come. You are coming closer to that time, as you do the work you are taking on.

Your process of awakening is beginning to bear fruit. You will be identifying synchronicity in your life. You are noticing how your life is guided by your thoughts and actions. The life you dream of can be yours. Trust in your intuition. It guides you.

What feels right to you, may not be right to others. Trust in what you sense to be right and true. Help who you feel guided to help. You are a Light to many. You are here in this world to help guide others to their own Light. Sometimes it seems obvious, other times not so much.

The time is soon upon you all, the time you have foretold, the time all are awaiting. You are doing all you can at this time to prepare. It will happen at the right time. Let go of expectations others are feeling/sensing. It is different for them. Your call is true, and your intuition to be trusted. It will be global in scale... effecting not just your world, but all the worlds around you. Let go of expectation. Do not let others' concerns and fears override commonsense and inner knowing.

Namaste.

Soul to the World

23   SPIRIT SUPPORTS

2021

I feel separated from my family. Have I created the separation or is there something real that I am sensing? (I seek comfort for the loss of family I've felt during Covid protocols)

You do sense your differences. It sets you apart in many ways. You feel deeply, and can sense differences in others, in their thinking, in the whys and wherefores. You can feel it all. Your family loves you, but they do not understand you. The separation you feel, they also feel. They do not know how to overcome it.

You need to release your family in love. They are taken care of. Your future does not belong with them. You belong to all. Your path is a hard one. It is often lonely. It is challenging, and only the very brave and courageous can take that path with you. For now, there aren't too many who can. Find a way to be ok with the loss of relationship to them. They aren't trying to hurt you...not purposefully. Jenny, you are on your path.... very much on it. You can't go backwards any longer. Only forwards.

When you are coming from a place of authenticity, as you do, you must be in relationship with those who are also. When they are not, you have a tough time connecting. You don't make small talk. It is awkward and uncomfortable for you. You do not seek to feel this way. Within your own family, you need connection. You have become much more in tune and in touch with your true Self. You cannot go back to pretending.

Some would say you are becoming more each day. Some would say that soon, there will be no choice for you than to always speak your truth to others, no matter the cost. You are finding navigating this space, in an authentic way, to be difficult. It will get better. There is a place for you in all of this. Being available to write and meditate is what you need to do right now. There is a purpose to your life. This is the time you have been waiting for. The time is now. Trust your intuition in how it is guiding you. Your thoughts, your beliefs, they are valid, they have wisdom, they are for this time. They are for these people.

This illness the others have created and spread; its time is ending. How humanity responds will be defining. Those awakening souls are growing larger in number. Soon they will overtake the dissenting voices. Soon they will number in the millions, in the hundreds of millions. For this is the time, Awakening is here.

We are legion, We are you. we are here for humanity, in Her rising. And so, it is.

24 PATH BEFORE ME

The messages of the next two chapters are more specific to me, but I share them because they speak of the time of my premonition. This message is for the entire world, and if 'they' are to be believed.... the time is coming very soon. I'm still not sure what role I am to play but can only trust what I am given. Perhaps you will find solace, hope and understanding in these pages.

2022

I was led to the first two books of Law of One, translated by Pamela Mace on YouTube over the course of a few weeks. The following are transcripts of channeling I received after listening to each part. I resonated so clearly with much of the material.

What density does my Higher Self reside in usually?

You are yourself a 6th Density (like RA)

Messenger?

Yes, you are a Bringer of Light.

Why did I choose to be born into a 3D life, with all the risks?

Because the need was great, and you believed you could do a lot of good.

Why is there so much sorrow for me?

You feel as humanity feels.

Why is my physical body struggling? (I had been bleeding steadily for a year, after a biopsy and many doctor appointments, found my body was working normally. Further confirmation this was spiritual in nature)

You are processing a lot of physical pain and grief, from your maternal generational line. You've processed the emotional aspect. You have processed the fear and rage. Now you process the blood.

How long have I been living/working my Purpose in this Life?

For a long time, since before birth. Your density is such where you can express your energy anywhere. Many know you by your energy. You are felt by so many. This is why your physical body gets so tired.

Why am I kept in unconsciousness?

Because to know our True Self, would overwhelm you. Soon you will.

Am I a Lightworker? *You are*

Am I a Messenger? *You are*

Light Bringer? *You are*

Tree of Life? *You are not*

6th Density? You are.

What percentage of me comes from my human soul? (I've had a growing sense that my human Self is completing its cycle, and my Divine Self is taking over. This may seem confusing to many. I am human, as we all are, but I am accessing more of my divine Self. We each can access this higher part of ourselves with preparation).

You are less than half, more of a fourth percent human. 25% yes.

Has it always been so, or less as I get older?

More (sixth) as you get older.

Why does my body vibrate?

You carry a lot of higher energy in you – this requires your body to hold it, it's an effort (causes vibration)

So, I'm approximately 25% human, 75% sixth? (A better rephrasing would be, that I am accessing over 75% of my Higher Self, and more as I get older).

And you are hoping to become full sixth in this life.

Am I on track? *You are.*

Why can I not access my Akashic Records, heal, etc.?

You can do those things when you have completely Become.

Can that happen in this life?

You are already Becoming.

So, souls are always striving to reach the One Creator, infinite Intelligence, moving from first to eighth density or more until becoming One again. To then start the process again....and this has gone on for infinity and will continue.

You understand most for now.

What is the Point, to infinity?

You can only understand as much as you do, until you can understand more. The Point is LOVE, in all its expression and Oneness.

Why cycle? Why not just continue?

Because the Source would know itself only as one aspect of oneness.

How many cycles has this universe been in?

Infinite.

How many cycles have I been on?

You have lived and become in so many.

Have I experienced Oneness with Source?

Yes, often, you yearn for it again.

These questions are huge concepts.

The fact you can ask them, and understand, speaks to your level of understanding.

What level of sixth am I?

You are getting closer to seventh.

how long have I been sixth?

Millions of years.

Has my human self-accrued any new karma in this life?

No, you always rectify it immediately.

Am I a 6th D wanderer?

You are both wanderer and sixth. You are not broken. You are more like a whole being now.

I am a RA wanderer?

No, you are a wanderer who came back to 3D to help humanity achieve its next level. You are RA so you can help bring messages to those who need them.

Who speaks?

You are the one who speaks. At the time of your transition, you are becoming your TRUE SELF.

Which is?

WOMAN Who asks God who you are, and the answer is...YOU ARE BORN TO BE SOUL TO THE WORLD

How can I be born to be a 'soul to the world?

You will Become your True Self. You are transitioning and when completed, will begin to prepare the way of Heaven on Earth. Jenny, you are here for many purposes. Your True Self is coming into your Full Self. You are preparing for that. You've been for a long time.

Are there others like me?

You are so sure you know who you are, but you do not know. You can say no to this Jenny.

After some time pondering...I say yes. If it is truly my path.

You know you are here for an important purpose. Your family supports you. Jenny, you are here for a purpose unlike any other. Your purpose is to become the True Soul of this world. There are many thousands here who are to bear witness and to support this mission. You are not alone. You are here to bear witness to the fullness of your Soul and of God. You are here.

Proof of this?

There can be no proof except as you experience. You are here for a Purpose and the purpose is soon to be upon you. You have welcomed your mission, and it is moving forward.

Is there any chance that I'm making this all up in my highly creative head? Born out of loneliness or ego.

No. No, this is all real and true. You are here to be witness to God. You can't imagine it. You can't fathom it. It is something you will experience, through what you will live.

Can I be shown evidence of this truth?

Yes, in messages meant for you, like videos, music, messages heard and seen and felt…. you will come to know the truth of this… and will come to accept it. (I read previous channelings from previous years. The evidence is there…they've been telling me of this for years!)

When I speak as 'Soul to the World,' what will my purpose be?

To provide strength and support for the harvesting (as referenced in Law of One). When human souls transition, (when they continue their Soul lessons and reincarnate), *they come back as fourth density. You have been sensing what is to come. Trust your intuition...trust what you are sensing. It comes from your Higher Self.*

One night, I received a message from Source walking me through a spiritual cleansing of my maternal family line from present to the ancient past and origination point. I visualized purifying their aura, their Merkabah, and Soul. We all shone with Light.

You are the hope of humanity. You can heal whole generations. You feel the depth of your power to change your own life and the lives of those around you with their given free will. Your healing gifts are given through emotions. Most chronic and fatal illnesses stem from disconnection and suppression of your (humanity) emotions.

What can I call this? What did I do within my own family?

Soul Healing.

(Most) toxicity comes through the mother's line. The nurturer. The power the dark receives from corrupting a mother's love is huge.

Once your work begins, families will recover, will grow, evolve, love again. You are healing the ancestors of the past, into the present. Release, Cleanse, Purify.

What does the healing look like?

Transformation., Lightness of Being. More expression of Love. The change that is 'spoken of' begins here. You are the One who knows. You are the One who can help heal this people.

I'm 6th density. I am here to help support humanity. I am the "Soul to the World," I will access and be living as my True Self when I Become. I'll be manifesting my true mission which is to help heal the souls of families and individuals. Is this right?

You are correct. Know it is always your free will to take this path.

I already chose it.

Yes, but living as a 3D consciousness, you must also give permission, and you have. You sense the times you are in. You always have. You will soon know how your meditation has worked in your family. Make yourself clear from the start, you are here to bring love, joy, and peace to the souls of the world. Only then can there be true Peace. It may take you and many others, lifetimes, but it will happen.

You will be made whole with your True Self. You will be made anew, and all will know of it. You will be renewed with purpose. You will know your True Self fully. You will remember every past life. You will make use of abilities you've dreamed of. Yes, your very life is a testament to how everyone can achieve the same.

You will bring hope to the world, where there is none. You are the perfect example and you volunteered to be this for the world. You have been prepared, all your life.

You are of a race of beings alike to Jesus; you came with love for humans and wish to help them see (the Way). You can be a Bringer of Love to the world by making yourself into a Lighthouse. You may not see it now, but many will be drawn to you and will be able to move into fourth density easier with your love.

What are the chances this is all ridiculous and a figment of my imagination?

You are the Light for (those) born again forever. You are the one who will be able to work with the Bringer of God.

How do I do this? I am just a human with problems, faults, passions, pain, joys, drama...just me.

When you become your True Self, when you become "Born Again" into a new world. Believe it Jenny. It is true. Because you have chosen this path. Believe you are here to bring the peace and love of God to the people of this world. This is why you are here. This is why you are.

What will this require from me?

You will be required to give over your whole self. Everything of yourself. You will become all that humanity has the capability of becoming. In ways you cannot fathom.

Will my children be safe and protected?

Yes, they have chosen to take this journey with you as your support.

I am consciously deciding/choosing the Path my Soul chose before this life. I commit to it. I know that my family is safe and protected. I know that those who are helping me on this journey are showing up right as they need to. I trust and know we are being taken care of. All our needs.

Believe it. you will become ready for this change. Your body will become a space that holds your immense Soul. Jenny, you represent the second coming that is within all of you.

Soul to the World

25 TRANSFORMATION

2022

I have begun my book.

> *You are following the Way as you know it to be, for now. Your words will have the ability to transform lives. You will know what it is like for others to experience your transformation. You will express it in a way that is relevant, and real for them. They will see themselves in your words and will come to know themselves., through you. This is why you are here; this is why you were born at this time, to share your own experience, and let others know about themselves. There will come a time when many will have read these books. Your words will have an impact on so many across the world. When the time comes, it will be accepted and known...and when you are in full Spirit, they will accept you. They will know Truth, and they will discover it for themselves. The time of harvest is almost upon this planet. Your work will help so many more reach the right level or place of spiritual unfoldment. Many who have been on the fence, will then find courage to become one with their true selves. You have no idea, jenny, the impact your*

words will have.

 Change is happening within. Like it has been for you... what you are experiencing, they are experiencing. Everyone has their own gifts, and the Messengers share as they understand. There are many, who "for your own good," are trying to influence others towards what they think is "right." They do not realize or appreciate that each human has their own path, and their own way to work towards healing and awakening. There is not a single way.... There are as many ways as there are stars in the heavens. You each have your own unique handprint...so does your Soul. There are similarities, yes, where one experiences resonance... and that is all we can hope for. Resonance, not dissonance.

 What is coming...

 Humanity is becoming aware and awake. More are sitting up and noticing what is really happening in the world. Less will be accepted. A Revolution of the Spirit is coming. It is building in crescendo...and everyone can feel it. You, you are the ones who will change everything. No outside force will do this. It will come from within. Do not listen to those who push fear propaganda. There is no "killer asteroid," 'alien invasion,' or "solar storm" that will wipe out humanity. These are tools of the dark, to instill fear. They feed off the fear. Always remember that...and tell others. These pandemics they have tried and failed to accomplish... they will try multiple times. They have lost the power to influence. People are taking stock and recognizing the truth for what it is. Avoid programming. Protect yourselves. (Live more in tune with nature, with each other, listen to your body's needs, trust your own way).

For those who awaken and wish to heal from the vaccines and boosters...they can do this. They can heal themselves or allow others to heal them. It will take courage... to speak up when you feel like your voice will not be heard or appreciated. Many are listening. Even within your families...they listen, even if they do not act like they do. The disconnection you all feel is the boundary you are feeling. You are still holding on to memories. You grieve the loss of what might have been in the past, but you need to recognize, you have never belonged to them.

Who speaks?

We are you...Metatron, Abraham, Jesus, Mary, you. Your higher self. WE are all here with you. Together. You are our Light, and with you we will Light the Way towards a beautiful new reality. It is all here...within them. They need the SPARK... and you are that Spark...you, and others like you.

Allow yourself to listen to Us...listen to your intuition...we are guiding you. You are guiding you. Do not worry about feeling connected to individuals. You are connected to ALL. Soon...you will know this.

And yes, your future.... you anticipate a Lightness of Being. You sense Joy in your future self. Let go of the how, and trust that you are guided. Trust we are showing you the Way and you yourself know this. Be the Way, we see within you. Release all doubts. All fears. You can never be disconnected from the True

Source...you are whole and part of It. Your human life... the life you identify as Jenny Kaefer Haag... she has lived up her life already. She has finished her first life. Now, you are living in the life of your Soul. Your family can sense this...your mother can sense the "otherness" of you. You are becoming "other," more...and that is as it is meant to be. Allow it to happen naturally. You will find when you stop resisting it, the peace that comes, and remains, will be profound.   The weight, the food, making yourself feel bad for your weight, for yourself. This is merely a distraction.

Am I walking the path of others before me? Those I might recognize? Something I can read to help me understand...to feel supported by?

Many in the LIGHT. You knew at an early age you would be following this Path. You were guided to that knowledge... you were also guided to knowledge your Path is unlike any other... there is nothing you can read to prepare you for where you are going... you can only live in each moment. Be present in the moment you are living. Let go of preconceived ideas of what "others" want for you. Do not be influenced by even your own children's expectations of who you are, or who you might be. They do not know, and that is ok....as it is meant to be. You are raising them to be strong, loving people. They are being prepared for their own path.

In the Light of Day, a time is coming when your words, your voice, will light a candle in the darkness.

Your writing... your peace, your Presence to each person

who is with you.... who can feel Me, with you. Jenny, you are being prepared for an immense journey into Spirit. Your heart is being prepared to be the light of joy to the world. Allow the peace of God to fall upon you. You are blessed in Me. I am here to speak through you and to bring the light of God into every single soul.

I am here for you God.

You are the one who I seek to use. You are the candle to my flame. You will be the single focused light in darkness. You are the Light of God standing before you. We are here with you, standing in your presence. Feel us.

What is coming God?

You are, we are One. They have no idea. They do not understand what is to be, they do not understand they are their own whisper, within their own souls. And you, you will be sending the Call. You are the one who will be showing the world how to live beyond what they see and live from their soul.

We are You. We are the Light of Man. We are the Way Shower. We are that to Whom you sing out to. We are here for you, and for all. There is no name, no label, which encompasses who we are. How would you define your true essence...because that is who we are.

We come to you, as You, to bring Light and awareness ... a return of your True Self, as you have not known yourself to be before. You have chosen to be here, in this body, in this family, in this home, in this city, in this region, on this planet, for a specific purpose. You are here to make ready, for that, which is coming...

which is almost upon you all. And you, you have known of this time.... you have prepared for this your whole life. When you look within, you know this. When you try to reason it out, using only your mind, and the expectations of those around you, you doubt yourself. You doubt what you know to be true.

You are a Way shower, here to bring Light to the World. You bring light to the world, through your very Presence. You bring Light, through your love, through your healing, through your willingness to take on that which is difficult. Your future is set, and yet you also have free will, to choose it for yourself. At any time, you can choose not to move in this direction. You can choose another direction...and it would be ok. As a soul, you choose your own way, your own path, as you intuitively sense you must.

And if I stay on this specific path...

Then you will become. Become all that a human is meant to be on Earth. You are to Become...to show the Way. Way Shower.

And to Become is?

You will transition into the Light of God and return in fullness of your Being. Holding the most a human form can hold, of the Light of God within you.

Humanity will wake more fully into their own truth. Into understanding, that each person can attain what you have. That eventually, no one will have to transition to achieve ascension.... that it will be a choice, and one will just be there.

Your driving force since you have become aware of your

true self, is to reach out to the "everyday" person....to share the Truth with them so they may have hope...so they may know this for themselves. To realize they, too, are of God/Source/Oneness...they, too, shine with love and light...they too, can ascend into a new life and out of the misery they created for themselves from ignorance, fear, hatred, sadness, loneliness, and society's influence; unaware of who they are. Believing they are separate from the One.

And they will see in me...?

One of their own. Not a celebrity, or a spiritual guru, or someone caught up in political maneuverings or greed. Someone who has always lived their life authentically, from a place of truth, even when others have belittled or doubted.... you never wavered from what you knew.

I am very human...with faults.

Yes, which is why it is you. Look within Jenny, you know what we say is true. Continue as you are. You are doing exactly what you are meant to be doing. And, as you write your book, more awareness and understanding will come to you.

You are Blessed. We are with you. There is coming a time in this world when what you have become will be exactly what the world needs. They need a respite. They need to breathe. They need to believe in goodness, hope, and love. Your creation...you answered the Call...of humanity.

Soul to the World

~EPILOGUE~

Many call the 21ˢᵗ century The Age of Information[52].   At society's level this is true, at a soul level, we are in the Age of Awakening. What are we awakening from? It is not simply unconsciousness to our true selves, but from the inherited belief "'it has always been and will always continue to be." Until the 1950's, we were mostly content to follow the rules, obey the one in charge, listen to what others told us was important, valuable, or safe. The revolutions during the 1950's and 1960's were revolutions of the Spirit. Across the world, people stood up for themselves, demanded acceptance and recognition for their individuality, and began fighting against 'the machine.' The global pot was vigorously stirred,

---

52   The Information Age, so named due to the creation and use of the World Wide Web and internet. The internet has made all information, knowledge and data available to anyone with the ability to have a computing device. This Age has democratized information, it has also flooded the world with misinformation and disinformation at much faster rates than previously, since it is delivered and made available in milliseconds. It requires education, a critical thinking mind and discernment to separate truth from fiction.

and all that had lain content on the bottom and top for thousands of years, were mixed all together. Our ancient longing for soul growth and change had reached Critical Mass and manifested gloriously.

Death is not glorious although inevitable, and war is a failure of diplomacy that ruins lives and hastens death all too often; however, they are important catalysts. The assassination of devoted proponents of Democracy and Non-Violence such as President John F Kennedy (1917-1963) and Martin Luther King (1929-1968) or the suppression of others like Nelson Mandela (1918-2013), and Mahatma Gandhi (1869-1948) had the opposite effect of their oppressors' intention, galvanizing revolution within the human heart. The Vietnam War did more to spur activism in the West, than it did to suppress communism within the country.

In the last seventy-five years, there has been more emotional and spiritual growth than at any other time in written history. Every single person on our planet, who has wrought positive change, or been a catalyst towards change, on the most micro or macro level, was born for this purpose. We've always been guided. We are never alone, and we are each born with a specific purpose, to discover over the length of our lives. We are being prepared for our next evolutionary leap of consciousness. People have been 'awakening' to the truth of their soul and purpose at an exponential rate, undergoing emotional battles and spiritual trials. They experience something they cannot explain and are sent down the rabbit hole of self-discovery.

Why does healing our emotional, mental, psychological and spiritual selves' matter? What is the point of awakening our True Selves? Why wake from the Matrix[53]? What does it all mean?

You picked up my book and others like it because you want answers, answers you have not yet received. Ironically, you already know the answers. We seek outside confirmation for what we know to be true. We experience resonance, when we read or hear words that seem to come from our own heart and soul. Perhaps you've experienced goosebumps while reading my book. Let them be a guidepost for your own journey and be willing to let go of whatever does not speak to you.

We've been conditioned our whole lives to trust 'others' who are in better authority to know. We start our lives trusting parents and caregivers, not realizing they only know what they have learned from others. In school, we are trained to think in an organized and practical way. We are trained out of our intuitive understanding of math, science, and the humanities. Children who achieve success

---

53   The Matrix references the Matrix trilogy of movies with actor Keanu Reeves, describing a shared simulation where most of the planet's humans are plugged in. Physical bodies are asleep, while their minds are awake in a dream state. They are caught in a repeating illusion.

with complicated numbers in their head are derided. They are told they must write it out so a teacher can trust they came to an answer correctly. Who is this for? It is to enforce a child cannot know their own self but must depend on someone else. It is conditioning. If the child is successfully trained and molded to follow directions, they graduate from academic institutions to join the work force, deferring their own intuition again, for those with better decision-making skills. Eventually (because suppressing our true selves over time can cause a crisis of the soul), we come to a reckoning in our lives. Do we continue trusting 'others' opinions, beliefs, advice, and recommendations, or do we stop and start listening to our inner self?

It takes tremendous courage to overcome lifetime conditioning and expectation from family and friends, religious institutions, society, careers, and our expectations of our life. When we begin the trek into our inner world, we stumble over the first stone. "Who am I?" or "Why am I here?" You begin reading everything you can, you listen to teachers, gurus and priests; you might take courses in intuition and meditation or sign up for spiritual weekend retreats. Books seem to leap off shelves, the 'right' person comes into your life to answer a question or point you in a new direction. You might have a supernatural experience you can't explain away. You start to trust yourself. You realize you cannot 'go back to sleep,' you know too much, so you must move forward. The awakening process is a grand adventure, giving depth and purpose to your life.

We are guided on our Path by our Guides and Higher Self. You may believe it is serendipity, fate, or luck. It is not. When you are on your life path, everything flows. When you step off your path, there are obstacles to overcome or be sidetracked by. No experience is wasted for our soul. Troubles may provide a needed lesson. Health challenges create opportunities for soul growth, either for us or those in our lives. Every major experience in our life has been planned before birth, by ourselves. Reincarnation is a real force, used by our Soul to continue its journey towards Oneness with Source. Most do not remember past lives, as that would interfere with lessons to be learned in this life. I have come to these truths through a lifetime study of the Human Spirit, near death studies, and communication with my own Higher Self and other Light Beings who are here to support and guide all of us to achieve Oneness (LOVE) with Source/God. We are here on Earth, a school for our souls, to express our love for each other in every possible way. To do this, we must let go of other's ideas of what that means. All the spiritual teachers and gurus in the world only know their own path and share it with us, in hopes we might find it useful in our own travels.

Until the 20th Century, humans went through a cycle of birth, karma, soul lessons, transition, reincarnation, repeat. From time to time, an Ascended Master like Yesua ben Joseph (Jesus), came to share with us how to speed up our process towards oneness with Source.[54] Every soul is at its own 'level' of awareness and works at its own pace. There is no point comparing your path with another for this reason. According to RA in the Law of One material, our souls are 'harvested' every 26,000 years to be reborn into our next density on an ascended Earth. December 21, 2012 was the approximate end to a 26,000-year cycle. We are ready for harvest. A Call was sent out by humanity to the 'heavens,' to help prepare us for ascension to fourth density. High density Light Beings, Wanderers, Star Beings, and Spiritual Guides answered the Call, choosing to incarnate into human life to support humanity. They are Lightworkers, Messengers, Way Showers, Archangels and more. Unlike the word harvest connotes, we will not be "reaped" like corn. It is a beautiful, natural, and instantaneous moment to be joyfully anticipated. It has nothing to do with Christian Rapture. You are not judged and found wanting. All can go. It is our evolutionary leap. Many have begun the process already. I am here to help support you on this journey.

A takeaway from this book, is this: We are here, on Earth, spiritual beings housed temporarily in physical bodies, to remember our True Higher Self, and then to live our lives

---

54   He spoke to us in 113 phrases found in the Nag Hammadi Caves in 1945. This text is called the Gospel of Thomas. After reading these words, sit with them and either accept or not. It is your free will.

with passion, focus, purpose and love. Do not focus on what happens after this life. Do not worry about when your soul is ascending or spend months and years of your life pursuing knowledge you already have within you. Live your life in the Now, fully aware. We are here to impact lives, to make a difference, to have faith, to live with hope, to believe in the infinite possibilities of our creativity and imagination. We are here to manifest a world we all want to live in. This is our Purpose on Earth. This is why we are all here.

I have re-read all my communication with Spirit for the past thirty plus years. The messages are consistent. I must trust the prophecy I was given in 1989. We seem to be living in those days, now. Something amazing is coming. We want it and our lives will be changed forevermore by it. Trust your intuition implicitly. It is your Higher Self and Source speaking to you. Trust the path you are on, even if it seems difficult or impossible at times. Spiritually, you chose this difficulty for the purpose of your soul's growth. Trust in that. Sometimes we need to just take one day at a time, or one hour at a time. I'm amazed every day by small and large miracles. Shift your focus, change your thinking from negative to positive. There are so many resources at our disposal. Ask and it shall be given. Prepare your body, mind and spirit for the next step in our evolution. I believe in you. I am here for you. I love you. Peace.

Soul to the World

ACKNOWLEDGEMENTS

Over the course of our life, through childhood, young adulthood, careers, jobs, health challenges, relationships, crisis and the messy everydayness of life, we may come to realize we are never truly alone. We are helped in every aspect of our life, by seeming bystanders. These are guideposts when we need guiding. Sometimes these bystanders become teachers, friends, lovers, catalysts, or mirrors to our own self. If we are fortunate, we come to recognize and anticipate them, understanding our meeting is not happenstance, but a mutual agreement to support each other for however long is necessary. If you keep yourself open to possibility, a random stranger in a coffee shop or bookstore can become a fellow voyager on a sea of dreams. I want to thank every single person I have met either on purpose, or through happenstance. You have helped direct my life, giving me purpose, focus, faith, and courage. While each one of you is important to my story, there are a few I wish to acknowledge here.

Before I understood the concept of Soul Tribe, I met Charlie Gibson and Linda Simek (Laney). While we met in high school, it wasn't until adulthood that our friendships truly took root and blossomed. With Linda, I learned about faith. I spent my youth mostly alone and forever dreamed of a best friend. I had unrealistic ideas of what that was, not understanding a true friend sees past our surface, past our struggles and pain, to what lies at the heart of us. It took me a long time to trust that she would remain after discovering my heart. She stayed, and we remain to this day, soul sisters. Thank you, Linda, for always being my friend.

After an initial six years of friendship with Charlie, we were separated by life for eighteen years. I never forgot him and through the years, would find us visiting in vivid dreams, chatting at a coffee house or his kitchen in San Francisco, or celebrating events at various places. When we found each other again, it was as if no time had gone by. When he shared about his life during that time, I was not surprised, as I already knew. Thank you, Charlie, for believing in this story. Thank you for reading it, for editing it, and providing the support I needed. You are my Anam Cara, and I am grateful.

I discovered maturity and adulthood while in a relationship and eventual marriage to my husband, Mark. Unbeknownst to both of us, I met and fell in love with him at the beginning of my spiritual awakening. With him, I've experienced every human emotion. With him, I discovered I am beautiful, worthy of love, and held to the Earth. He is my anchor, my mirror to my true self, my agony and my incredible joy. He is unwavering, loyal, incredibly patient and a cheerful early morning riser. Without him, I would not be who I am today, and for that I am forever grateful. Even though he does not understand who I have become, he is always there for me. I see you, Mark. I know you and I love you.

Dad, you have been my rock and foundation. Despite health concerns, international business travel, and the incredible soul challenges you've undergone through your life, you have always been there for me. There is a steadfastness to you, which I always try to emulate. You've raised four wonderful, emotionally strong, and courageous women. You helped to form us into who we are today, and for that (and of course, our weekly gin rummy games), I am forever grateful. Thank you for being my father in this life. Thank you for loving me with everything you have.

Words cannot convey the deep well of love and gratitude I hold for my mom. Together, we chose to tackle generational trauma within this family. We each had our missions and found the fortitude to carry them out while in amnesia to our true selves and of our Soul Purpose. We have healed this family to the point of origin, and out into the far reaches of its future. Momma, you have been my confidante, my dream weaver, my inspiration and staunchest supporter. With you, I have uncovered courage, acceptance, forgiveness, unconditional love and compassion for myself, my family and all of humanity. Dad created my foundation; you have always been my home. Thank you for choosing me as your daughter. Thank you for believing in my writing ability, encouraging me to 'find my voice' and for your guidance through every step. This book would not exist without you.

Kathy Kaefer (Dickey), thank you for being my biggest fan. You believed in me at a time when I didn't believe in myself. You were always my protector, my confidante and loving childhood playmate. A Rosebud needs Sunshine to thrive, and you always were that to me. You've always believed in and encouraged my writing, as I have always believed in you. Thank you for choosing me as your big sister. Your vivid shining light bathes us all. I love you.

~Annie Kaefer (Bernstein), you were the one who gave me *Conversations with God Book 1*, by Neale Donald Walsch. This book was instrumental during my spiritual awakening. In that gift, I knew you understood who I was becoming. I have always known the deep love you hold for me. I am grateful for the gift you are in my life. I have always loved you. I have always been proud of you.

Elizabeth Kaefer (Sweetman), the quiet anchor in our family. Your peaceful presence enhances every gathering. My 'little Beth,' always there to provide love and companionship. Like mom, you've followed the Healer's path. I appreciate all you have done 'behind the scenes' to support and love us all. Your quick wit, excellent party planning skill, and keeper of all common sense, endures. Thank you for being there for me during my son's prolonged illness. I love you.

Others who deserve recognition include my close friend 'Stella Mochel, steadfast, loyal, and fellow parent of a cancer survivor. You made that necessary journey so much easier, thank you! I'm grateful to my older friend and mentor, Sonda Cotes - artist extraordinaire, who introduced me to Dr. Wayne Dyer's wisdom. Thank you to Art Bell from Coast-to-Coast Radio, for believing me and confirming my intuition all those years ago! Thank you A'lan Danmar for encouraging me to listen to my inner voice and Higher Self. To the owners and crew at Fair Oaks Coffee House and Deli, in Fair Oaks, California, thank you for providing a warmhearted space for my writing, endless cups of delicious coffee and enlightening conversations with patrons and staff.

Thank you to fellow writers Sarah K. Grace (*Journey Into Grace; Tales of a Psychic Paramedic*), Dr. Wayne Dyer (*Your Sacred Self*), and Matt Kahn (*Whatever Arises, Love That*) for inspiring me with your honesty and truth. I've been privileged to get to know each of you and through your inspiration and encouragement, have continued my journey, knowing I am led to a wonderous place of self-healing, grace and unending joy.

Soul to the World

BIBLIOGRAPHY

Aron, Elaine and Arthur, *The Highly Sensitive Person: How to Thrive When the World Overwhelms You*, Published by Broadway Press, copywrite 1996

Bradshaw, John, *Homecoming: Reclaiming and Healing your Inner Child*, Published by Bantam Books copywrite 1992

Cannon, Dolores, *Jesus and The Essenes*, Published by Ozark Mountain Publishing copywrite 1992, 2009, *The Three Waves of Volunteers and the New Earth* Published by Ozark Mountain Publishing copywrite 2011

Dyer, Wayne W. Ph.D., *Manifest Your Destiny*, Published by Harper Perennial copywrite 1997, *Your Sacred Self*, Published by William Morrow Paperbacks copywrite 2001

Grace, Sarah K., *Journey Into Grace: Tales of a Psychic Paramedic*, Published by Dry Leaf Press copywrite 2016

Joy, W. Brugh, M.D., *Joys Way: A Map for the Transformational*

Journey, An Introduction to the Potentials for Healing with Body Energies, Published by J.P. Tarcher, Inc. copywrite 1979

Hawkins, David R., M.D., Ph.D. *Letting Go, The Pathway of Surrender*, Published by Hay House, Inc., copywrite 2012

Hay, Louise, *You Can Heal Your Life*, Published by Hay House, Inc. copywrite 1984, 1987, 2004 and *Heal Your Life*, Published by Hay House, Inc. copywrite 1998

Hicks, Esther and Jerry, *Ask and It Is Given: The Teachings of Abraham*, Published by Hay House, Inc. copywrite 2004

Kahn, Matt, *Whatever Arises, Love That: A Love Revolution That Begins with You*, Published by Sounds True copywrite 2016

Kennedy, Russell, M.D., *Anxiety Rx: A New Prescription for Anxiety Relief from the Doctor Who Created It*, Published by Awaken Village Press copywrite 2020

Kryon, *The Twelve Layers of DNA*, Book 12, Published by The Energy Extension, Inc. Published by Platinum Publishing copywrite 2010, *The New Human: The Evolution of Humanity*, Book 14, Published by The Kryon Writings, Inc. copywrite 2017

Moorjani, Anita, *Dying To Be Me: My Journey From Cancer to Near Death, to True Healing*, Published by Hay House,

Inc. copywrite 2012

Orloff, Judith, M.D., *The Empaths Survival Guide: Life Strategies for Sensitive People*, Published by Sounds True copywrite 2017

Redfield, James, *The Celestine Prophecy: An Adventure*, Published by Warner Books copywrite 1993

Virtue, Doreen, Ph.D., *The Lightworkers Way: Awakening Your Spiritual Power to Know and Heal*, published by Hay House, Inc. copywrite 1997 and *Chakra Cleansing: Awakening your Spiritual Power to Know and Heal*, Published by Hay House, Inc. copywrite 1998

Walsch, Neale Donald, *Conversations with God: An Uncommon Dialogue, Book 1*, Published by Putnam Books copywrite 1995

Soul to the World

RESOURCES

(Healing) Anger

Tipping, Colin, *Radical Forgiveness: A Revolutionary Five-Stage Process to Heal Relationships, Let Go of Anger and Blame, and Find Peace in Any Situation* Published by Sounds True copywrite 2010

Aromatherapy

www.healthline.com/health/what-is-aromatherapy

Awakening Symptoms

www.ashleymelillo.com/blog/19-stages-symptoms-spiritual-awakening

Constellation Family Therapy

www.hellinger.com/en/,

Wolynn, Mark, *It Didn't Start with You: How Inherited Family Trauma Shapes Who We Are and How to End the Cycle* Published by Penguin Publishing Group; Reprint edition (April 25, 2017)

Manne, Joy, Ph.D., *Family Constellations: A Practical Guide to Uncovering the Origins of Family Conflict,* Published by North Atlantic Books copywrite 2009

Emotional Freedom Technique

Craig, Gary, EFT Tapping Points, free eBook at www.emofree.com

Ortner, Nick and Dr. Mark Hyman, *The Tapping Solution: A Revolutionary System for Stress-Free Living,* Published by Hay House, Inc. copywrite 2014

Energy Cord Cutting

https://goop.com/wellness/spirituality/cord cutting-for starting-over/

Emotional Detox

Boyle, Sherianna, MED, CAGS, *The Emotional Detox: 7 Steps to Release Toxicity and Energize Joy,* Published by Adama Media copywrite 2019

Energy Healing/Reiki

health.clevelandclinic.org/reiki

Brennan, Barbara Ann, *Hands of Light: A Guide to Healing Through the Human Energy Field,* Published by Bantam New Age Books copywrite 1987

Epigenetic Inheritance

Golden, Ronald, *Epigenetics and Trauma. How Epigenetics can potentially revolutionize our understanding of the structure and behavior of biological life on Earth,* Published by YouCanPrint copywrite 2021

(Recovering from) Fear

https://www.oshoteachings.com/category/osho-on-fear-fearlessness/

Dr. David Hawkins *Map of Consciousness* (see Bibliography)

Functional Medicine

www.drhyman.com

Hyman, Mark, M.D., *Young Forever: The Secrets to Living Your Longest, Healthiest Life* (The Dr. Hyman Library, 11) Published by Little, Brown Spark copywrite 2023

www.ultrawellnesscenter.com

Global Peoples Assembly

www.globalpeoplesassembly.org

Ho'oponopono Prayer

www.hooponoponomiracle.com

Law of One, RA Material

McCarty, Jim and Carla Rueckert (transcribers), *The RA Contact: Teaching the Law of One Volume 1 & 2*, published by L/L Research copywrite 2018

Mace, Pamela, video translations of *Law of One Book 1, 2, 3, 4*, www.youtube.com/@pamelamorinegypt

Life Between Life Studies

Newton, Michael, Ph.D., *Journey of Souls: Case Studies of Life Between Lives*, Published by Llewellyn Worldwide copywrite 1994, 1995, 2005 and *Destiny of Souls: New Case Studies of Life Between Lives*, Published by Llewellyn Worldwide copywrite 2006

Medical Intuition

Grace, Sarah K., *Journey Into Grace: Tales of a Psychic Paramedic*, Published by Dry Leaf Press copywrite 2016, 2022

www.suehannibal.com, an excellent description of what medical intuition is, and how it is used

Relationships

Chapman, Gary, *Relationships: The 5 Love Languages: The Secret to Love that Lasts*, Published by Northfield Publishing copywrite 2015

Spiritual Planes, Dimensions, Densities

Initiation with Matias De Stefano, GAIA TV

Understanding Oneness

Rasha, *Oneness*, Published by Earthstar Press copywrite 2003

Soul to the World

ABOUT THE AUTHOR

Jennifer lives in Northern California with her three beautiful children, loving husband and ridiculous French Bulldog. She earned a bachelor's degree in Anthropology and completed graduate work in International Affairs from CSU, Sacramento. She spent the first half of her working life in nonprofit organizations, with an ardent desire to help others and the second half as an educator in her local school district. She has written a blog on WordPress since 2013 chronicling her spiritual discoveries www.soultotheworld.com and is active on most social media sites. She became aware of her own True (Higher) Self over the course of thirteen years after experiencing several spiritually transformative experiences (STE) which catapulted her self-healing and spiritual growth. She has been in communication with ascended masters, her spiritual guides and Higher Self, where they have shared with Jennifer, her real identity, purpose on Earth, and how she is to help humanity recognize and achieve their full potential as spiritual beings. She is spiritually Ascended and here as Lightworker to help others find their own way towards their True Purpose and become everything they are intended to be.

She welcomes letters and email and will try to respond to each one. Reach out to her Facebook page @ SoulToTheWorld email: soultotheworld@gmail.com, http://Amazon.com/author/soultotheworld